I0882953

The Magic Mirror of Literary Translation

The Magic Mirror of Literary Translation

Reflections on the Art of Translating Verse

Eric Sellin

Syracuse University Press

Syracuse University Press
Syracuse, New York 13244-5290

First Edition 2021
21 22 23 24 25 26 6 5 4 3 2 1

∞ The paper used in this publication meets the minimum requirements of the American National Standard for Information Sciences—Permanence of Paper for Printed Library Materials, ANSI Z39.48-1992.

For a listing of books published and distributed by Syracuse University Press, visit https://press.syr.edu.

ISBN: 978-0-8156-3703-5 (hardcover)
978-0-8156-3711-0 (paperback)
978-0-8156-5517-6 (e-book)

Library of Congress Cataloging-in-Publication Data

Names: Sellin, Eric, 1933– author.

Title: The magic mirror of literary translation : reflections on the art of translating verse / Eric Sellin.

Description: First edition. | Syracuse : Syracuse University Press, 2021. | Summary: "In "The Magic Mirror of Literary Translation," Sellin examines and dissects a number of his translations in a detailed series of ten essays that consider the importance of the various elements involved in the practice of literary translation, especially when it comes to dealing with potential roadblocks that can frustrate a translator of highly structured formal poetry"— Provided by publisher.

Identifiers: LCCN 2020020741 (print) | LCCN 2020020742 (ebook) | ISBN 9780815637035 (hardcover) | ISBN 9780815637110 (paperback) | ISBN 9780815655176 (ebook)

Subjects: LCSH: Poetry—Translating.

Classification: LCC PN1059.T7 S45 2020 (print) | LCC PN1059.T7 (ebook) | DDC 418/.041—dc23

LC record available at https://lccn.loc.gov/2020020741

LC ebook record available at https://lccn.loc.gov/2020020742

Manufactured in the United States of America

Contents

Acknowledgments

I extend my thanks to the editors of the following journals in which some of this material first appeared, and I am grateful to them for their interest and encouragement.

"Poetic Compromises and the Uncertainty Principle: Translating Verhaeren's 'Le Navire'" first appeared in *Metamorphoses* 20, no. 2 (Fall 2012), 122–33; my translations of Charles Baudelaire's "The Albatross" and "The Cracked Bell" first appeared in *Ezra: An Online Journal of Translation* 7:1 (February 2013); and my translation of Baudelaire's "An Icarian Lament" first appeared in *Ezra* 11:1 (Winter 2017), no pagination.

"The Translator as Critical Whistle-Blower" first appeared in *Metamorphoses* 21:2 (Fall 2013), 164–67.

Chapter 6 ("'Free Verse'; Free of What?") consists largely of revised portions of an earlier essay, written for *World Literature Today* ("Letter from the Near East and the Maghreb," *WLT* 57:1 [Winter 1983], 55–58), in which the interesting discussion with Mahmoud Haider and Husnī Farīz, recorded with their knowledge and approval, was first published.

Introduction

Some Rules of Engagement in Literary Translation

I do not intend with these essays to enter the sometimes heated debate going on these days between advocates of rhyme and meter in poetry and those who consider formalism obsolete and believe that it might just as well be eradicated from the canon. I have written both formal and free verse for more than sixty years and I see no need for either of these forms of poetic expression to be excluded from the writer's kitbag of available devices.

Many of the young aspiring poets of my generation worked at mastering their craft, inspired on several fronts by the discipline of poets like Ezra Pound, Theodore Roethke, Richard Wilbur, and others; by the open free verse and field poetics of William Carlos Williams, Charles Olson, and E. E. Cummings; by the alliterative and musical energy of poets like Gerard Manley Hopkins, Hart Crane, and Dylan Thomas, and some of the dithyrambic texts of Allen

Ginsberg and other poets of the Beat Generation; and by the haiku whose technical nuances had been popularized by Donald Keene and others and that we toyed with in order to hone our skills at handling imagery and metaphor.

The trajectory of my own poetic adventures led me from a predilection for structured formal poems toward several decades devoted mostly to free verse, followed by a return to form in recent years. Furthermore, from my earliest undergraduate days to my most recent projects, I have uncompromisingly labored at composing formal literary equivalencies, or "translucencies," of scores of rhymed metrical poems that I translated from French and Italian. To produce a good translation of poetry, whether in rhyme and meter or in free verse, the translator must also be—or at least aspire to become—a good poet for the occasion.

So what constitutes good poetry? I would suggest that poetry is found in a virtual no-man's-land between, on the one hand, the clippity-clop of mechanically rhymed verse of the sort more legitimately used in circumstantial, satirical, or mock verse and, on the other, the headlong stampede of unbridled free verse. The Real Poet worthy of that title lives more or less in isolation in this no-man's-land yet somehow manages, when necessary, to infiltrate the two neighboring domains to smuggle out some of the undeniably useful but unrefined resources found in both domains and which the good poet will know how to exploit to help create a dynamic tension between rigorous restraint and spontaneity in his or her own work.

Perhaps, in the interest of full disclosure, I should also issue an alert regarding the genesis of these essays and the kind of audience for which they are intended. Upon retiring from a career in Academe I found it difficult at first to refill my lungs with the fresh air of the real world and to take up primary creative and intellectual activities that had often been stifled or repressed during those years behind ivy-covered walls. For several post-retirement years I felt the need for some sort of decompression as I tried to reorient and reprogram my life and my abiding interests.

I found much-needed relief in the interesting and gratifying challenges of writing formal verse, in revisiting and revising some old poems that I realized were in need of mending, and especially in translating sundry formal French masterpieces that others had previously tackled with varying degrees of success.

In the essays that make up this collection, I preferred to put behind me the brand of writing requisite to advancement in an academic career and opted instead for a style more commonly associated with the familiar essay. Readers may think that here and there I have gone over the top and become earthy, scatological, or bumptious; I would ask that the reader forgive me such moments and attribute them to the few stray nitrogen bubbles that my giddy ascent had failed to eliminate during my gradual decompression and normalization, processes that these episodes of translation and analytical commentary helped to enable.

The essays are to some degree self-sustaining and may be read either in sequence or in random order. Although dealing with serious matters, these essays are meant to be entertaining as well as instructive. An interesting discovery that I made upon emerging from the regimented and sometimes stultifying world of Academe was that literary translation, once considered hack work by many scholars, had recently become prestigious and that the formal poetic muse was making a genuine comeback.

Early in my career a friend wrote to urge me to submit my candidacy to fill a faculty vacancy at his university in California. He closed his letter with the advice that I should list only my academic publications, omitting any reference to my own poems and poetry translations. He suggested that a record of a book and a dozen articles would have a greater impact on the hiring committee than any number of scholarly publications *plus* poems and translations published in journals and chapbooks. Unfortunately, for many people a poet is deemed irrelevant, or even worse. Consider two telling comments drawn from Dennis O'Driscoll's delightful *Quote Poet Unquote: Contemporary Quotations on Poets and Poetry.* Gwyneth Lewis strings a cordon sanitaire around the poet, claiming that "[i]n England, if you say you're a poet, it's as if you have a personal hygiene problem"; and as Christian Bök quips: "Unlike other work, being a poet is a culturally demeaned occupation. It's not the kind of thing I'd use as a pick-up line. Saying you're a famous poet is tantamount to saying you're a famous croquet player."[1]

Upon retirement I was pleasantly surprised to find an esthetic and intellectual climate in which theories of literature had become truly global, multilingual, and transnational, a climate in which translation had been revalorized and was now considered an important creative and intellectual activity. I felt as though my many years spent translating poetry under the counter, so to speak, had been vindicated.

The familiar and occasionally irreverent style of these essays reflects the genuine pleasure I have found in returning guiltlessly to the translation and retranslation of metrical rhymed poems, a passion I have long harbored but which, as I just stated, has only recently been acknowledged at large to be a worthwhile one.

Some theorists claim that all language, indeed all art, is a form of translation; others maintain that a successful literary translation is to some extent a transcreation and is actually an instance of coauthorship by the original author and the translator. The very notion of translating a master poem into

1. Dennis O'Driscoll, *Quote Poet Unquote: Contemporary Quotations on Poets and Poetry* (Port Townsend, WA: Copper Canyon Press, 2008), 79.

another language has long been the topic of much discussion, the cynics having maintained over the years that translation is tantamount to betrayal (*Traduttore, traditore!*), plagiarism, or simple self-serving laziness. Many would rightfully reject the idea that A's translation of "Sonnet X" is better than B's; or that C's version of that sonnet is the best ever. The words "better" and "best" only serve to remind us that such value terms function not only as modifiers qualifying the end product but also as semantically loaded terms that reflect the eye and mind of the reader or beholder who assimilates the end product as well as the original text if the reader is fully conversant with the latter's language and its cultural and literary traditions.

In these essays, my solution to the dilemma of dealing with the many uncertainties involved in literary translation has been simply to ignore those uncertainties and to concentrate on snagging the brass ring while enjoying the merry-go-round ride of the translation process; and then to focus my attention on the actual translation process . . . treacherous though it might be.

My title, *The Magic Mirror of Literary Translation*, is meant to suggest the relativism and uncertainty inherent in any translation, especially in verse translation. The Disney-esque phrase behind my title (namely, "Mirror [or Magic] Mirror on the wall, who is the fairest one of all?") suggests several convenient interpretations. A mirror yields a reversed and possibly distorted encoding of original objects; and the modifier "fair" may be glossed as "pretty" or "becoming" but also contains by inference such synonyms as even-handed, just, light-skinned, or average and mediocre. Even my subtitle is a punning truth-in-packaging label, for these essays are themselves reflections in the dual sense of mirror images (perhaps skewed ones) and intellectual musings (drawing on an evanescent stock of friable memories).

Finally, I am grateful to a number of friends whose opinions I respect and who have shown their support and encouragement, thus making the whole undertaking seem worthwhile and, of course, all the more fun to pursue as I strive with all my might to be an agent worthy of my source poets. My special thanks go to Thalia Pandiri and Peter Thompson, who liked and published some of these essays and translations in their journals; to Peter Krok, who liked and asked to reprint two of the *Ezra* translations from Baudelaire in *The Schuylkill Valley Journal* after I had read them at the Manayunk-Roxborough Arts Center; to Hédi Abdel-Jaouad, Mohamed Kamara, and the late Robert W. Greene, who read several of these essays and gave them a much appreciated thumbs-up; and to Mbarek Sryfi who slyly lured me into mining the rich new lode of contemporary Arabic-language poetry and who has, during our many interesting sessions co-translating Moroccan poets, amiably put up with my rudimentary Arabic and my pedantic cavils concerning such grammatical details as false or ambiguous antecedents and how one might most properly translate various examples of the tricky *iḍāfa* (إضافة) genitive construction.

But now let us get on with the game! Croquet, anyone?

Philadelphia, 2019

THE MAGIC MIRROR OF LITERARY TRANSLATION

1

Poetic Compromises and the Uncertainty Principle

Translating Verhaeren's "Le Navire"

My students, faced with an assignment to translate a paragraph from French to English and no doubt concerned about obtaining a satisfactory grade, often asked just how literal the translation should be! My standard answer was that a good translation is faithful to the original in content *and* intent. This axiom will apply whether one is dealing with a scientific treatise or with a highly creative work, such as a lyric poem. In many translations, fidelity to the *content* is paramount (Think rocket science, medical alerts, and DIY assembly instructions accompanying toys or furniture shipped from abroad!); but the more "literary" and creative a source text becomes, the more the translator will feel obliged to accommodate the *intent* of the author and to convey certain elements above and beyond the mere didactic or informational data. It is a matter of adapting to the translation act the symbiosis between form and function.

This element of intent may become formal and aesthetic to such an extent that the onus is on the translator to find ways, in the target language, to remain faithful to the raw content of the original while also attempting to "carry over" the author's manifest artistic intent. In such translations it is not enough to know the original language; one must also bring into play various technical skills (in, say, the composition of rhyme and meter) as well as sensitivity to such things as musicality, rhythm, and alliteration. For example, a translator may find it easy to translate Balzac adequately yet be quite stymied when it comes to rendering the idiosyncratic mechanics of a novel like Georges Perec's *La Disparition* that is composed entirely of words without the letter *e* or capturing the haunting style of, say, J. M. G. Le Clézio's *Les Gens des Nuages* or *Désert.* (I recently read C. Dickson's translation of *Désert* and it is a tour de force in its successful transcreation of the ineffable poetic cadences of Le Clézio's descriptive prose.)

The challenge faced by the translator of poetry is particularly rigorous when the merits of the original lie primarily in its structural and stylistic "ineffables." Some poetry, like that of 2011 Nobel Prize laureate Tomas Tranströmer (1931–2015), relies heavily on the engine of imagery to achieve its desired effect. One critic, commenting on the award, made note of the highly effective "torque" of Tranströmer's juxtaposition of disparate images. Many, many translators, myself included, have more or less successfully translated the Swedish poet into English since 1966 when Tranströmer's "Fifteen Poems" appeared in *New Directions Annual* no. 19. I once wrote that Tranströmer's work had attracted so many translators and been translated into so many languages (some 60 at the time of this writing) largely because his work is relatively easy to translate since metrical rigor and musicality are secondary to the cognitive imagery in his poems, allowing one to translate them into other languages with "minimal aesthetic heat loss."

If a poem owes much of its power to such things as interesting rhymes and off-rhymes, consonance and assonance, rhythmic effects such as alliteration (e.g., Gerard Manley Hopkins, etc.), unusual metrical architectonics (e.g., Victor Hugo's "Les Djinns"), musical overtones (e.g., the melancholy lines of Verlaine's "Chanson d'automne," laden as these are with mournful nasals and liquids), stirring resonances, even overblown rhetoric, then the fidelity to intent may very well find itself in conflict with the obvious desideratum that one retain the basic propositional content of the text.

Let me offer an anecdotal example of how this tug-of-war between the message and its "ornamental vehicle" or medium might play out—sometimes over many years—as the translator tries to negotiate a settlement of the conflict even as he or she realizes that there will inevitably be compromises favoring one of these adversaries (this being a given of the stock and trade of the literary translator) and occasionally instances of absolute incompatibility (in which case it is probably wiser to abandon the project).

All my life I have been fascinated by ships and the sea. As a boy I read all of C. S. Forester's Captain Hornblower novels and memorized Ariel's full-fathom-five song in *The Tempest*; and in recent years I have read and reread all of Patrick O'Brian's Aubrey-Maturin sagas. In my twenties I worked coastwise on an oil tanker and sailed in a twenty-six-foot sailboat from Sweden to Finland with my brother. It is only natural that I should be attracted to poems, such as those by John Masefield and Roy Campbell, that are able to evoke the grandeur of such adventures.

It is no surprise, then, that I was attracted to "Le Navire" by the French-writing Belgian poet Emile Verhaeren (1855–1916). The poem, published in Verhaeren's 1910 collection entitled *Les Rythmes souverains*, consists of six quatrains of alexandrines in crossed rhyme (abab) and offers the reader no significant narrative, reminding one rather of a traditional romantic painting of a majestic sailing ship. If there is any didactic subtext, it is to be found in obvious metaphorical abstractions concerning things like the ship of state, a firm hand on the helm, the unanimity of a common cause, "staying the course," and so forth.

I translated the poem in the early 1960s and I thought I had caught its essence and that it sounded just right when read aloud. I had given it my best shot and, with just a slight twinge of unease over some of the compromises I had resorted to in order to retain the poem's "music," I relinquished "The Ship" to the undergraduate literary magazine at Temple University, where I was teaching at the time.[1]

The poem's virtue resides in the beauty of the description of the ship itself and the bonding with those magnificent universals of sea, sky, and stars. The text tells no story as such and to succeed the poem relies heavily on its intent rather than its content or cognitive data. A good translation of "Le Navire" would have to render the rhyme and meter and capture the sense of lofty, mythic grandeur in the poem's resonance. That, for better or worse, had been my goal.

After I retired in 2001, I started going over my old material, often making revisions. In a spin on a famous Mark Twain quip, the observer affected the observed. I found that this author/translator in his seventies seemed to be wiser than he had been in his twenties and thirties and no longer carried away by adolescent exuberance. I also now found myself at a certain remove from some of my earlier "baggage" (including impetuosity and not a little arrogance) that may have made me fail to take the time and make the effort to apply the final bit of mental "elbow grease" needed for an optimum result.

In going through those old writings, I came across and reread my translation of "Le Navire" and was immediately bothered by *something*. I could not put

1. *Stylus* 10, no. 2 (Winter 1966–67): 24.

my finger on just what, but I determined to identify and remedy the problem, if possible.

When I now approached the poem, not as an enthusiast of nautical lore nor as a poet trying above all to achieve a faithful reproduction of the metrics and the stirring musicality of Verhaeren's poem, but as a craftsman, I immediately realized that in several sections of the poem I had been so intent upon conveying the creative elements in the original that I had allowed the rhyme and the tone of the poetry to prevail over the content and over some factual givens that were at the very foundation of the poem, notably nautical and astronomical accuracy! In one particular compromise I actually came across as an utter landlubber!

The problems that no doubt had caused my unease some fifty years ago are, I believe, to be found in the second and third stanzas of my translation; and the root cause was actually my having committed one of the cardinal sins of which translators of rhymed metrical poetry are often guilty. Over the years, translators of texts like *The Iliad*, *La Chanson de Roland*, and the *Divina Commedia* have settled for everything from prose versions of rhymed epics to conversions into blank verse or a modified stanzaic or rhyming system, acknowledging, as it were, the difficulty in retaining the original's full poetic panoply. Some manage nicely by maintaining in the translation a feel for the original without emulating its form one hundred percent. Thus John Ciardi successfully translated Dante's *terza rima* (aba/bcb/cdc, etc.) into tercets more loosely linked (axa/byb/czc, etc.), largely ignoring the leapfrogging rhyming of the end-word of the second line with the first and third end-words of the subsequent tercet, a pattern that gives the original a quasi-crossed-rhyme effect. Translators often radically transpose the structure of the original into a format more recognizable to readers of the target language and possibly one that they, as practicing poets, are more comfortable with; so alexandrines are turned into iambic pentameter, couplets are turned into quatrains with crossed or shackled rhyme, terza rima into octosyllabic quintains, and so forth.

In my effort to transpose the full effect of Verhaeren's poem, I retained his crossed rhyme scheme but opted for iambic pentameter, the Anglo-Saxon equivalent of the alexandrine.

The first stanza came out well and I thought I had it made, so to speak. It seemed to be reasonably true to the content and to convey a fair amount of the music of the original:

> We slid forth calmly underneath the stars,
> The slanted moonbeams played about our lee,
> And the tall white tower of sails and spars
> Cast its vast shadow out over the sea.

> Nous avancions, tranquillement, sous les étoiles;
> La lune oblique errait autour du vaisseau clair,
> Et l'étagement blanc des vergues et des voiles
> Projetait sa grande ombre au large sur la mer.

Perhaps I was counting my chickens before they had hatched, for I proceeded to stumble through the next two stanzas before recovering my pace in the last three. It now is obvious to me that the "unease" I felt years ago after first translating the poem was due to my failure to maintain, in the second and third stanzas, the sense of *inevitability* that marks virtually every good translation.

Let me analyze these two stanzas, the challenges they presented, the initial "compromises" (or blunders) made in order to accommodate such formal exigencies as rhyme, and, finally, the newer version in which I try to rectify these deficiencies. Here, then, are those two stanzas in the original, each stanza followed by my defective first version from the early 1960s:

> La froide pureté de la nuit embrasée
> Scintillait dans l'espace et frissonnait sur l'eau;
> On voyait circuler la Grande Ourse et Persée
> Comme en des cirques d'ombre éclatante, là-haut.

> The cold purity of night consumed us,
> Shone out in space and shivered on the waves;
> We saw the Big Bear turn, with Perseus,
> In games of shadows bursting from their graves.

Commentary

The problem in this stanza involved the idea of the "cirques" that obviously means zones, areas of activity, and not "circuses," and especially the lure entailed in the quest for appropriate and glowing rhymes. I loved having to find a rhyme for "Perseus" even if in the process I had to slightly skew the content, suggesting that "we" were consumed whereas the word "embrasée" obviously modifies "night"! But my momentum got out of control when I put the word "waves" on paper, a flourish that irresistibly led me to contrive the lovely rhyme in the last line. That final flourish sounds magnificent; however, in rereading it with a cold objective eye, I realized that the last line is not only meaningless but is patently absurd. It seems more suited to the Big Bang than to the nightly journey of the constellations. We have here a prime case of form and adornment riding roughshod over content. In my 2010 revision I have tried to restore some sense of the astronomy at play in the original although I no doubt took other liberties to maintain the rhyme ("aurora borealis" and "Perseus").

It was in the third stanza that I took complete leave of my senses and found myself playing nautical roulette, not realizing how it could mortally wound the poem. It is one of the weaker stanzas in the original French, but it is loaded with enough seafaring terminology to excite my imagination and make me run amok. The opportunity to make verse out of such nautical items as *le mât d'artimon* (foremast), *le mât de misaine* (mizzenmast), and *l'avant* and *l'arrière* (fore and aft), as well as the marine phosphorescence suggested by the stern and bow wakes *où se dardaient les feux* (where lights darted) was irresistible to me, even if the last two lines are rather pedestrian:

> Dans le mât d'artimon et le mât de misaine,
> De l'arrière à l'avant où se dardaient les feux,
> Des ordres, nets et continus comme des chaînes,
> Se transmettaient soudain et se nouaient entre
> eux.

> In the foremast and in the mizzenmast,
> From poop to prow where sea-sparks darted,
> The orders, sharp and steady like chains cast
> In the blue, were called as we departed.

Commentary

This first version of stanza three at first seems to make sense, but once again I had lost sight of the content as I played with the nautical references and then tried somehow to jazz up the last two lines, with disastrous results. Just read the above stanza aloud and it will become obvious that one poorly selected word was sufficient to have scuttled the whole poem and cause the malaise I had felt over the first version. Poop? Good Lord! At the time I had wanted to retain the aft-forward word order of the original so that the phosphorescence would be in the bow wave rather than in the stern wake. This antecedence would occur in the alliterative "poop to prow" or the awkward inversion "stern to stem" (the phrase is normally "stem to stern"), but that "poop" had to be eliminated, that's for sure. In revising the stanza, I hesitated between the alliterative "stem to stern" (phosphorescence flashes occur in stern wakes as well as in bow waves) and the more literal "stern to bow," losing the alliteration but also jettisoning that "poop" word. Ultimately, I picked "stern to bow" and went on to the Herculean chore of salvaging the last two lines, possibly saving the very ship itself from sinking.

As I have already mentioned, this is a weak stanza and the didactic thrust of the last two lines—promoting solidarity and "unanimism"—lulled me into a degree of inattention to contextual detail. The original image uses the cast-iron chain of orders shouted out as a metaphor for authority and united effort, but it is somewhat guilty of mixing metaphors when it brings in the verb *nouer* (to tie or knot together), a word that suggests ropes and hawsers rather than chains that one does not knot. In an attempt to give some coherence to these two lines, I altered the basic image: "Des ordres, nets et continus comme des chaînes, / Se transmettaient soudain et se nouaient entre eux" became, in my first version, "The orders, sharp and steady like chains cast / In the blue, were called as we departed." Unfortunately I had slipped in some "data" that by inference would lead one to conclude that the tall ship was under the command of a nincompoop (and here the word is appropriate). In maintaining the integrity of the meter and the rhyme, I had created two ambiguities: "cast" suggests "cast in iron" but here clearly means "cast" in the sense of thrown out. This idea, which should be an analogy of sharp commands (the chain of command, if you will), is further skewed by my next ill-advised use of the phrase "in the blue." Those words were meant as mere metrical filler! The only time you would cast a chain in the blue (viz. the sea) would be when dropping anchor. To make matters worse, the impervious translator/captain then, for the want of a better rhyme, went on to state " . . . as we departed."

The general impression I had created was that as the ship was leaving port the captain dropped anchor! Even the worst landlubber should be able to foresee the disastrous result of such a maneuver. There would be, at the very least, some torn timbers or a demasting, at the worst a foundering with the loss of all hands.

Conclusion

Had Jacques Rivière, the editor of the *Nouvelle Revue Française*, not snatched the most recent revision of Paul Valéry's "Le Cimetière marin" from the poet and published it forthwith, Valéry would no doubt have continued to revise it, sometimes radically. And let us remember that many a poem or translation will benefit from revision after some delay. Perhaps the old argument that literary masterpieces like the Bible, *Don Quixote*, the *Divine Comedy*, the *Iliad*, *The Song of Roland*, or *A Thousand and One Nights* need to be retranslated periodically in order to remain relevant may find a parallel on a smaller scale in the lifespan of one translator. The translator will, perforce, evolve as an observer with his or her times, and his or her "take" on the object of contemplation will consequently evolve, too.

Finally, I like to think that I have improved my translation of Verhaeren's "Le Navire," but I know that every translation is subject to its own *uncertainty principle* and, even as I now relinquish this revised translation for publication, I do so with just a twinge of unease.

The Ship

Emile Verhaeren

Translated from the French by Eric Sellin

We slid forth calmly underneath the stars,
The slanted moonbeams played about our lee,
And the tall white tower of sails and spars
Cast its vast shadow out over the sea.

The cold purity of the aurora borealis
Glittered in space and trembled on the main;
And, high above, the Big Bear and Perseus
Made the nightly rounds of their domain.

In the foremast and in the mizzenmast,
From stern to bow where sea-sparks danced,

Orders, sharp and steady like chains cast
In sturdy links, were shouted out as we advanced.

Each seaman aided as we swiftly rode
The sea, lending an instant of his force,
And the wave, bearing up both keel and load,
Gave the men strength and bore them on their
 course.

Immensity embraced the brigantine
Whose stem traced out long wakes where fishes
 dwell;
The rigging shuddered like a tambourine
For him who held her close-hauled on the swell.

She pitched above the ghastly, death-deep mud,
In harmony with each star in the night,
Taming the united elements as though some blood
Coursed through her stays, eternal in its might.

Le Navire

Emile Verhaeren

Nous avancions, tranquillement, sous les étoiles;
La lune oblique errait autour du vaisseau clair,
Et l'étagement blanc des vergues et des voiles
Projetait sa grande ombre au large sur la mer.

La froide pureté de la nuit embrasée
Scintillait dans l'espace et frissonnait sur l'eau;

On voyait circuler la Grande Ourse et Persée
Comme en des cirques d'ombre éclatante, là-haut.

Dans le mât d'artimon et le mât de misaine,
De l'arrière à l'avant où se dardaient les feux,
Des ordres, nets et continus comme des chaînes,
Se transmettaient soudain et se nouaient entre
eux.

Chaque geste servait à quelque autre plus large
Et lui vouait l'instant de son utile ardeur,
Et la vague portant la carène et sa charge
Leur donnait pour support sa lucide splendeur.

La belle immensité exaltait la gabarre,
Dont l'étrave marquait les flots d'un long chemin.
L'homme qui maintenait à contrevent la barre
Sentait vibrer tout le navire entre ses mains.

Il tanguait sur l'effroi, la mort et les abîmes,
D'accord avec chaque astre et chaque volonté,
Et, maîtrisant ainsi les forces unanimes,
Semblait dompter et s'asservir l'éternité.

2

Translating Old Chestnuts, or Who Needs Another Version of Two Oft-Translated Poems by Charles Baudelaire?

As mentioned in the previous essay, I have in recent years been spending considerable time revising old poetry manuscripts and working on translations. Over the past sixty years, I have published translations of hundreds of poems but for many of those years I harbored and struggled with an old prejudice—one no doubt handed down to me by my academic mentors—that assumes translation to be an activity lower in the creative hierarchy than original literature and, perhaps more nefariously, considerably lower on the Academic totem pole than scholarly writing; consequently I had some difficulty appreciating the significance of the recent surge in Translation Studies and Theory.

Now that I have once again become deeply immersed in translation, I have begun to understand and appreciate several elements that have been emerging in this field. I am convinced that the new importance attributed to the act of translation—notably the intense engagement in the intertextual and intercultural action that translation entails and that is championed by Edith Grossman, Lawrence Venuti, Dana Gioia, and others—is a very healthy phenomenon. The primary beneficiaries of this refocusing are poetry and textual criticism alike. The trend seems to have emerged from the ashes of the AOCT (Age of Overarching Critical Theory) and appears to be bent on restoring sanity to textual analysis and on recognizing, once again, the validity of authorial intent and cultural givens inherent in the source text as well as many important factors at play in the composition of the translation.

I have found the translation of formal verse particularly interesting and rewarding as you would no doubt have surmised if you have taken the time to read the preceding essay in this book. Recently I made English adaptations of two oft-translated old chestnuts by Charles Baudelaire ("L'Albatros" and "La Cloche fêlée"), translations that first appeared in Peter Thompson's *Ezra: An Online Journal of Translation* 7, no. 1 (February 2013).

I suppose the first question that may occur to one when contemplating these efforts is: Why on earth would you feel the need to undertake yet another translation of these famous poems by the greatest of the French Symbolist poets when scores, if not hundreds, of translations of those texts already exist? Well, the decision to render those poems into English derived not from any obvious public need or cultural urgency but rather from my own decision to use the rigorous analytical process inherent in a careful aesthetic translation in a personal quest for a deeper and more acute appreciation of Baudelaire's originals. The ultimate reward would be to somehow transcend time, cultural boundaries, and linguistic frontiers and to live, for a moment, in the original poet's immediate world.

By using this devotional approach to the Baudelaire poems, I became so involved in retrieving the creative impulses of the originals' aesthetic givens (their rhyme and meter, rhythm, alliteration, and extraordinary imagery) that the resulting English versions seem to me to stand well alone and have, I am glad to report, been appreciated by a number of friends whose critical judgment I respect.

After completing my translation of "L'Albatros," I went online and looked at translations of this poem by such great translators as Roy Campbell, Richard Wilbur, and Norman R. Shapiro. I was particularly interested in studying the compromises they had obviously made in order to convey not just the descriptive and didactic content but also the aesthetic intent of the poem.

There are, in each of those translations as there no doubt are in mine, distracting idiosyncrasies and omissions. Ambiguity is a hallmark of Symbolist poetry and compression seems to be an inevitable by-product of any translation that would preserve an original's rhyme and meter, even if English versification, unlike the French, allows for considerable expansion and abbreviation of line length. The French use of nominal adjectives in the singular (*un blessé*, *un mort*, etc.), for example, may require additional, often awkward, syllables in English (a wounded man, a dead person) or a different word like "casualty" or "corpse." Furthermore, to accommodate these extra syllables one may be required to eliminate other syllables in the poem.

Sometimes a word in the original text might be changed or added primarily in order to achieve rhyme or to maintain metrical integrity, but at other times the change or addition may provide a descriptive clarification that may, in turn, derive from the translator's relative interest in or knowledge of the original text's subject matter. A translator who fancies ornithology might very well choose different words in translating "L'Albatros" than would an amateur sailor whose only experience would be, perhaps, that he had read "The Rime of the Ancient Mariner." And a translator who is a pipe smoker or pipe collector may linger more on his rendering of "brûle-gueule" [literally a "mouth burner" or "mug scorcher," that is, a cutty or short-stemmed pipe] than would a nonsmoker, although anyone who has smoked a pipe or watched someone smoking a pipe will understand that the natural gesture of pointing or poking with a pipe would be by holding the bowl and pointing with the stem, as opposed to the hammering gesture entailed in tapping the ashes or embers out of the bowl of a pipe.

While wrestling with my translation, I contemplated and experimented with elements that might be expendable in the original poem and/or eligible for inclusion in my translation. My use of "skiff," a word also used by other translators, is obviously dictated by the quest for good rhyme, even if a "skiff" can be either a rowboat or a small open sailing craft. I figured that this ambiguity didn't matter a great deal since the category of vessel would be clarified by the reference to oars ("avirons"):

> Their large white wings droop pitifully, bent
> Down by their sides like the oars of an
> abandoned skiff.

I then agonized over my use of the adjective "abandoned," which, unlike the word "skiff," is not suggested even by inference in Baudelaire's original; but the more I thought of it, the more the adjective seemed appropriate. My rationale for selecting that word, aside from such consideration as euphony or rhythm, would be one of fidelity to the fundamental metaphor (drooping, cumbersome, hindering wings = oars that are in some way analogous to those wings) and the assumption that if the skiff were manned and underway, the oars would be moving synchronously; and if the skiff were stopped, the boatmen would presumably have been told either to "rest on their oars" (holding them in a horizontal or upward-slanting position) or to "ship their oars" by laying them fore and aft inboard. The word "abandoned" in itself suggests "empty" but also "disarray," as though there had not been time to stow the oars and make the skiff shipshape. In addition, the notion of abandonment conforms to the overall theme of the poem: the birds' and the poet's loss of identity and purpose when they find themselves out of their element or comfort zone. Now, after considerable deliberation over this adjective that does not even occur in the original French, I decided that the word "abandoned" was only marginally more suggestive of a backstory than the word "empty" and that, although admissible through standard English metrical license, "abandoned" tended to make the line in which it occurred sound and appear too long. So I ultimately opted for the visually and aurally less intrusive "empty":

> Their large white wings droop pitifully, bent
> Down by their sides like the oars of an empty
> skiff.

Over the years it had never occurred to me to translate Baudelaire's "L'Albatros"—partly because it had already been capably translated by many poets and scholars—but recently a friend threw down a gauntlet of sorts by showing me his literal version of the poem. Having recently completed translations of

Verhaeren's "Le Navire" and "La Barque," published respectively by *Metamorphoses* 20, no. 2 (Fall 2012) and *Measure: A Review of Formal Verse* 7, no. 1 (2012) I found myself on something of a roll and I decided to meet the challenge by attempting my own verse translation of "L'Albatros."

The poem that followed "L'Albatros" in the anthology I had turned to for Baudelaire's original was "La Cloche fêlée," a poem whose first stanza I had for years used to illustrate for students how the power of alliteration and musicality could be masterfully manipulated to great onomatopoetic effect. I had never dwelled much on the entire poem, which had always left me somewhat cold, but I have since the 1960s never ceased to find the poem's first quatrain, especially the first three lines, awesome:

> Il est amer et doux, pendant les nuits d'hiver,
> D'écouter, près du feu qui palpite et qui fume,
> Les souvenirs lointains lentement s'élever
> Au bruit des carillons qui chantent dans la
> brume.

Now, the qualities I especially admire in this stanza are firstly the aptness of the poet's use of consonants, reinforced by alliteration, in the second line (D'écouter, près du feu qui palpite et qui fume), and secondly the way in which the true onomatopoeia in that line (the consonants being reminiscent of the crepitations of a fire log crackling and popping) is contrasted with what I like to call abstract onomatopoeia in the first line (the clear open vowels of "amer et doux" contrasting grandly with the somber long *i*'s in "nuits d'hiver" or the interaction of the sumptuous sibilants and languorous liquids of the third line (Les souvenirs lointains lentement s'élever).

Having just plodded through my twenty or so versions of "L'Albatros," I decided to try my hand at translating "La Cloche fêlée," certain that I could never replicate these much-admired effects. Indeed, I had to settle for an alternate version of the fire, capturing the fricatives of the original in "flickering fire" but opting for a fire's hissing sibilance rather than attempting to convey the inimitable crepitating concatenation of labiodentals and plosive bilabials in Baudelaire's original (D'écouter, près du feu qui palpite et qui fume).

Unable to do justice to the mood created in the marvelous third line (Les souvenirs lointains lentement s'élever) in which the two fricatives have been downgraded from *f*'s to the less invasive *v*'s and the two audible sibilants have been dominated by the six nasal consonants and vowels and the four evenly cadenced liquids, I compromised and rather concentrated on the meter and the context of the image in the third line, remanding any sibilants or liquids to the second line. (Examples of such retrofitting during revision are also found in the reversal of images, analogical tropes, or grammatical clauses in several other stanzas in these two translations.)

On a wintry night it is both bitter and sweet
To sit by a flickering fire's hissing log
And to hear dim ancient memories become
    discrete
With the ringing carillons that peal in the fog.

I am not particularly happy with my rendering of the second and third lines of "La Cloche fêlée." It has been claimed that the most harmonious lines in French poetry are found in Racine's tragedies in, say, Hippolyte's description of Phèdre ("La fille de Minos et de Pasiphaé") or Oreste's lament to Pylade that it has been his fate to "traîner de mers en mers ma chaîne et mes ennuis"; but, as melodious as these lines may be, they provide little associative energy between their content and their sounds. The past master of expressing images and ideas in pertinent wording and musicality was, no doubt, Victor Hugo, but obvious candidates for the most successful lines in French poetry should include Paul Verlaine's "Les sanglots longs / Des violins / De l'automne / Blessent mon coeur / D'une langueur / Monotone" and the opening quatrain of Baudelaire's "La Cloche fêlée." Once again we need to remember that a good translation may be a great literary contribution and have noble aesthetic attributes of its own, but that a translator cannot and should not aspire to clone an original and that ideally we should also try to read and savor the original poem, if we can.

Almost every word, line, and image of a formal poem presents the translator with challenges of the sort discussed in the preceding paragraphs. I like to keep the revisions of my translations, at least until I have published the text. I have never made a formal count, but I would estimate that when I translate a poem composed in free verse I go through some four or five drafts. When I translate a poem in blank verse or in rhyme and meter, such as the two presented here, I revisit and revise the text on average about twenty to twenty-five times. First I make a photocopy of the poem and then I make a draft translation in the margins of that photocopy, sometimes changing this crude draft five or ten times. During this first phase, I tentatively sketch out some of the original's rhyming and other technical assets, and the final version on this page becomes nearly illegible. I type up that version, which often will include at least one stanza that is already nearly finalized, and then I make some revisions on the computer and then more on a printout (thank God for computers!). This process is repeated five or six times, sometimes entailing restoration of previously discarded elements, until I have a version that I feel is presentable in English and reasonably faithful to the original. I am then ready to publish it or share it with readers; however, I have never finished a translation without a vague feeling of inadequacy, a sense of having not quite nailed the brass ring of whatever it was that attracted me to the original poem in the first place. But the purpose for the preceding remarks is to underline the difference in the challenges of translating free or formal verse: the statistics involved in the relative rigors of composing and revising the translation of a formal structured poem as opposed to a text in free verse are, at least in my case, significant—a ratio of about five-to-one!

I find the current resurrection of formal poetry and the valorization of rigorous translation inspiring and long overdue. But, as Dana Gioia has pointed out,

> There is a danger in doing too much translation. When you translate, you always know where you are going. The original poem provides you with a map. But writing your own poems is a far more mysterious process. The poem is invisible until you write it down. There is no original, only impulse and intuition. It's hard to make the transition from translation back into original work.[1]

Of course, the poet who is translating will have brought to that task some of his or her own "impulses and intuitions," and yet Gioia's point is well taken. And I suppose it does suggest that there may, after all, be something of a hierarchy or at the very least a symbiosis involving on the one hand the creation of an original poem and on the other the translation of an

1. Dana Gioia, "Poetic Collaborations: A Conversation with Dana Gioia," *World Literature Today* (Sept–Oct 2011): 30.

existing poem, even if the source poem was conceived in a language different from that of the translator/poet. In short, if you want a poem translated find someone who knows the original and target languages but who is also a poet whose own impulses and intuitions are worthy of our attention. And, if the original is in rhyme and meter, make sure the translator is ready and able to make the many revisions that will most likely be needed to achieve a satisfactory translation.

The Albatross

Charles Baudelaire

Translated by Eric Sellin

Often, the ship's crew members, just for sport,
Snare albatrosses, the broad-winged sea birds
    that sweep
Majestically high above the sailors far from port,
Lazily following the vessel as it slides over the
    deep.

As soon as these kings of the bright blue
    firmament
Are trapped upon the deck, clumsy and stiff,
Their large white wings droop pitifully, bent
Down by their sides like the oars of an empty skiff.

How weak, how awkward this winged voyager is!
Once most beautiful, now ugly and absurd!

One sailor pokes at its beak with the stem of his
Pipe; another, limping, mimics the once soaring
bird.

The Poet is quite like this prince of the heavenly
spheres—
A denizen of mighty storms, indifferent to
stalking
Archers—for once on the ground amidst catcalls
and jeers
His gigantic wings prevent him even from
walking.

L'Albatros

Charles Baudelaire

Souvent, pour s'amuser, les hommes d'équipage
Prennent des albatros, vastes oiseaux des mers,
Qui suivent, indolents compagnons de voyage,
Le navire glissant sur les gouffres amers.

À peine les ont-ils déposés sur les planches,
Que ces rois de l'azur, maladroits et honteux,
Laissent piteusement leurs grandes ailes blanches
Comme des avirons traîner à côté d'eux.

Ce voyageur ailé, comme il est gauche et veule!
Lui, naguère si beau, qu'il est comique et laid!
L'un agace son bec avec un brûle-gueule,
L'autre mime, en boitant, l'infirme qui volait!

Le Poète est semblable au prince des nuées
Qui hante la tempête et se rit de l'archer;
Exilé sur le sol au milieu des huées,
Ses ailes de géant l'empêchent de marcher.

The Cracked Bell

Charles Baudelaire

Translated by Eric Sellin

On a wintry night it is both bitter and sweet
To sit by a flickering fire's hissing log
And to hear ancient dim memories become
discrete
With the ringing of carillons pealing in the fog.

Indeed, how fortunate is the full-throated bell—
Alert and hale despite its old age lament—
Steadfastly uttering its faithful knell
Like an old soldier on watch calling out from his
tent.

As for me, my grieved soul is cracked and longs
To people the icy night air with its lively songs,
But its feeble voice merely resembles at best

The muffled death rattle in the heaving chest
Of one who has been wounded and then left
where he lies
Beneath a pile of corpses where in agony he dies.

La Cloche fêlée

Charles Baudelaire

Il est amer et doux, pendant les nuits d'hiver,
D'écouter, près du feu qui palpite et qui fume,
Les souvenirs lointains lentement s'élever
Au bruit des carillons qui chantent dans la brume.

Bienheureuse la cloche au gosier vigoureux
Qui, malgré sa vieillesse, alerte et bien portante,
Jette fidèlement son cri religieux,
Ainsi qu'un vieux soldat qui veille sous la tente !

Moi, mon âme est fêlée, et lorsqu'en ses ennuis
Elle veut de ses chants peupler l'air froid des nuits,
Il arrive souvent que sa voix affaiblie

Semble le râle épais d'un blessé qu'on oublie
Au bord d'un lac de sang, sous un grand tas de morts,
Et qui meurt, sans bouger, dans d'immenses efforts!

3

The Translator as Critical Whistleblower

The recent surge in literary translation has reemphasized the very close critical reading required if a translator is to understand and convey even a small portion of the art brought to the original by its author. The translator is forced to make profound critical decisions, often needing to unsnarl ambiguities that may work well unchallenged in the original language but must be clarified in proper idiomatic English or fail altogether; or needing to decide which elements to save and which to jettison when forging a parallel poetic structure and/or rhyme scheme.

When laboring over a translation of a rhymed sonnet, sometimes one becomes not only aware of the difficulties in remaining true to the propositions of the original when creating a gracefully rhymed discourse, but also realizes that, in fact, the original contains areas of poor workmanship or betrays a facile abandonment of meaning in order to achieve harmonious end rhymes.

I have been revisiting some of the old classic poems I studied and admired in college. This retrospection necessarily brings with it another evolved viewpoint; sometimes poems that I once found very moving now seem awkward, even ridiculous. I should like to consider one such poem, Ronsard's famous sonnet to Hélène, "Quand vous serez bien vieille, au soir, à la chandelle" (1578), which today comes across as poorly made and replete with vainglorious persiflage.

I decided to make a translation of the poem and then compare it to some existing translations. My idea was simply to have fun and to undertake an exercise, a kind of solfeggio, to practice my intellectual and poetic scales. I ended up making several quite distinct versions of Ronsard's poem, one of which is provided here.

While undertaking this in-depth analysis of the original text, I became aware of certain weaknesses, some of which may be attributable to the fact that the poem was written at a time when French was just developing as a refined language of high literature and was still subject to irregular grammatical conventions and the need for neologisms of the sort recommended by Joachim du Bellay in his *Défense et illustration de la langue française* (1549). An example of what might have constituted expedient or creative ambiguity in Ronsard's syntax is the line "Regrettant mon amour et votre fier dédain," wording that may have gotten by in the mid–sixteenth century but today is inadmissible as the two direct objects ("amour" and "votre fier dédain") are both dependent on the verb "regretter," which, however, assumes different pragmatics for each object. "Regretter" first means "to miss" or "long for" and in the second linking means "regret," "rue," or "be sorry about"; Ronsard's line is thus akin to a phrase of the sort Strunk and White would condemn: "He was good at playing the piano and possum."

What happened next I find quite interesting. I was not content with trying to clarify the syntax and ambiguities in the sonnet; I also became annoyed with Ronsard's arrogance and lecherous agenda. I was fully aware that such "seduction" poems were common in Italian, French, and English poetry during the Renaissance, but I still found myself empathizing with the women whom these male chauvinist Lotharios would crassly suborn. If the poets had paid more attention to their craftsmanship, perhaps they would have had to do less pleading!

In short, I found myself writing a response to Ronsard in defense of young Helen's virtues and panning Ronsard's egoistic assertions. The triptych of Ronsard's original, the fairly literal translation, and my reply to Ronsard is thus meant to be read as a single transcultural, translingual, and chronologically osmotic experience.

Sonnet pour Hélène: Quand vous serez bien vieille . . .

Pierre de Ronsard (1524–85)

Quand vous serez bien vieille, au soir, à la
    chandelle,

Assise auprès du feu, dévidant et filant,
Direz, chantant mes vers en vous émerveillant:
"Ronsard me célébrait du temps que j'étais
belle."

Lors vous n'aurez servante, oyant telle nouvelle,
Déjà sous le labeur à demi sommeillant,
Qui au bruit de Ronsard ne s'aille réveillant,
Bénissant votre nom de louange immortelle.

Je serai sous terre et, fantôme sans os,
Par les ombres myrteux je prendrai mon repos;
Vous serez au foyer une vieille accroupie,

Regrettant mon amour et votre fier dédain.
Vivez, si m'en croyez, n'attendez à demain:
Cueillez dès aujourd'hui les roses de la vie.

A Sonnet for Helen

Pierre de Ronsard

Translated by Eric Sellin

When you are old, seated in the evening by the
fire,
By candlelight carding and spinning your wool,
You shall recite my verses and, marveling,
admire
How Ronsard sang your praises when you were
beautiful.

Not one of your servants, though having labored
so hard
And now half-asleep, shall, hearing that phrase,
Not start awake upon learning that the great
Ronsard
Had glorified your name with his immortal
praise.

Under the ground, a boneless empty phantom,
I shall lie, taking my rest in the myrtle kingdom,
While you, an old crone hunched near the fire's
glow,

Shall pine for my love and rue your proud
disdain.
Enjoy life now! Don't wait till tomorrow in vain!
Pick life's roses today; do so right now!

To Ronsard

Eric Sellin

Let's say that you'd gone to the fireplace,
Too old to walk without your knobby cane,
And joined good Helen where she sat and tatted
lace,
And she smiled at you without the least disdain;

And you were dumb-struck by her youthful
looks
Defying time so well that all your books

Seemed to drone like one long platitude
Compared to her unflagging pulchritude.

And all her tired servants nodded half-asleep,
Dozing through your paean's every peep
And wheeze and groan about her radiant light.

Surely you must have understood down deep
That though in verse you were to bray all night
This was one flower you would never reap.

4

Translating Formal Poetry versus Free Verse

A Specimen Sonnet by Du Bellay

In other chapters I have spoken of the hopes and expectations one might harbor of "nailing" a verse translation through meticulous work and thoughtful revision. I do believe I have possibly done just that in my several renderings of poems by Charles Baudelaire and Émile Verhaeren. There are, however, times when one seems to have achieved at best a journeyman performance with an adequate but less than superlative translation; times when the only option remaining is between settling for a personal best or abandoning the text altogether.

Composition of a mediocre verse translation may be the result of any number of factors, including the nature and relative value of the raw material one has to work with; one's own skill—or lack of it—in coping with the hurdles particular to any transposition of a given original into the second language; or even such negative input as fatigue or a personal aversion to aspects of the original poem's content or imagery.

Upon careful comparison, an awkward product in English may actually turn out to be a faithful reflection of the original text's inadequacies; and perhaps that is why poets seem to prefer retranslating a famous poem to translating a lesser poem by a great author or a fairly good poem by a mediocre author. Of course, one does not always have a choice, as when trying to translate an epic poem like *The Odyssey* or an entire collection of poems like *Les Fleurs du mal.* Not all translations will work out equally well, just as all of an author's own poems will never be equally successful. The famous "Sonnet pour Hélène: Quand vous serez bien vieille . . ." by Ronsard is not without its weaknesses, as I mentioned in chapter 3. The same may be said of many of the poems of Joachim Du Bellay. I have always thought Du Bellay to be a more endearing and personable poet than Ronsard and I had the urge one evening to "process" one of his poems.

I chose one of Du Bellay's most famous poems and thought it would be reasonably easy to translate. Despite my many drafts and revisions, I remain unconvinced that my translation does the original justice. I have to admit that my effort is probably at best an uninspired effort even if I found the process personally rewarding in that the translation required a close reading of Du Bellay's poem, because as one translator has remarked: "You never read a text more closely than when you translate it."[1]

One should keep in mind the fact that in this chapter I have ended up not focusing on the creation of an all-surpassing version of Du Bellay's well-known poem "Heureux qui, comme Ulysse, a fait un beau voyage . . ." (*Les Regrets*, Sonnet XXXI) but have rather focused on the very process of revision that is so critical in the "transcreation" of any poem, especially one in rhyme and meter. This chapter is not, then, about a translation but about the translation process per se.

Having composed poems in formal and free verse under intellectually focused as well as rhapsodic or intoxicated circumstances for some sixty-five years, I can attest to the fact that, in my case at least, the dynamics of creativity and the rigors of rewriting and perfecting a poem are quite different when it comes to free verse and formal verse. I like to suppose that this is an obvious given!

In this essay I would like to share with the reader some reflections on those rigors involved in formal composition as they come into play in the translator's attempt to convey both a formal poem's content and its formal eccentricities. Without the latter, some very

1. Steven J. Stewart, "Through a Veil: Some Propositions Regarding Translation," *Translation Review* Issue 91 (2015): 28.

well-known poems would become little more than didactic or narrative information.

I have found that the same importance that revision assumes in creating an "original" formal poem, say a sonnet written in one's own language, holds true when one is hammering out an acceptable equivalent to such a poem written in another language. It may be that the exigencies imposed on the poet's muse by the contract he or she has made with formality are even more restrictive when the target poem dictates additional demands of its own. Certainly a successful translation of a poem in free verse requires a degree of hard work and personal talent, but my own experience has been that—just as original free verse often spontaneously molds itself to the cadences of the creative impulse that spawned it—the translation of a free-verse original allows a more spontaneous "translucence" in which the content may be faithfully rendered while the music is successfully transposed into the new language with riffs and tremolos of its own.

I would estimate that the average free verse translation takes me through three or four revisions (constituting emendations of anything from a full revamping to the changing of one or two words) and that the average formal verse translation (whether in rhyme and meter or in blank verse) entails about twenty-five revisions, from rephrasing whole sentences to changing one word. Some of the revisions actually reincorporate syntax or locutions that had been found wanting in earlier drafts.

In general, I have found that in free-verse translations I tend to put far more emphasis on the tone and message of the original text with a good bit of syntactical and rhythmic alteration to accommodate my personal poetic "druthers" and to make the poem take on a life of its own in English. On the other hand, when translating rhyme and meter, I find that most of my sweat, tears, and chicken-scratching on the pages of drafts bespeak a genuine effort to recreate the formal music of the original verse or a variation thereof that will provide the rewards one derives from a good rhymed and metrical poem. If one is not a born rhymester, one must make numerous drafts and experiment repeatedly with word choice and order if one hopes to come up with a result worthy of the original.

It is also worth pointing out once again that very few poems in the history of literature—no matter how famous they might be—are without imperfection. In chapters 2 and 3, I have addressed weaknesses in several masterpieces by Ronsard and Baudelaire.

I had never understood why people thought "The Albatross" was so great and I hoped the very close reading of it that twenty or more revisions would entail might lead to a more favorable appreciation of the poem. On the other hand, I have for many years enthusiastically taught "The Cracked Bell," gushing over its opening quatrain, a stanza I consider one of the finest bits of poetry in literature due to its multiple levels of literal, alliterative, and onomatopoetic brilliance. I always felt that whoever tried to translate that stanza was doomed to failure. I gave it a try and discovered that, once past the first half-dozen lines, this masterpiece contains lines that are rather ordinary.

Rare is the poet who can sustain an opus without some sort of flawed music, grammar, syntax, or imagery. Just like the formalist poet, the verse translator sometimes has to make concessions and compromises. One should not necessarily try to improve lulls or defects in the original. But in practice, shortening or sacrificing altogether a weak line may give the translator a little latitude to play with the rhyme or meter to meet the needs of a more memorable passage in the poem.

I would like now to share some of the actual dynamics involved in translating formal verse, using as my example Joachim du Bellay's famous poem "Heureux qui, comme Ulysse, a fait un beau voyage . . ." (*Les Regrets*, Sonnet XXXI), a text in which the poet speaks of his homesickness for his native land. It was of no importance that the poem has already been translated many times. What was of interest to me was the very process of coming to grips with the poem intensively over a two-week period and trying my best, by any and all means, to do justice to the original and recapture almost kinetically some of the impulses that inspired Du Bellay four-and-a-half centuries ago. Here is Du Bellay's poem with modern French spelling. For those interested in such relics, the poem in its mid-sixteenth-century French spelling is reproduced in the appendix, along with drafts of my translation of Sonnet XXXI.

> Heureux qui, comme Ulysse, a fait un beau
>   voyage,
> Ou comme celui-là qui conquit la toison,
> Et puis est retourné, plein d'usage et raison,
> Vivre entre ses parents le reste de son âge!
>
> Quand reverrai-je, hélas, de mon petit village
> Fumer la cheminée, et en quelle saison
> Reverrai-je le clos de ma pauvre maison,
> Qui m'est une province, et beaucoup d'avantage?
>
> Plus me plaît le séjour qu'ont bâti mes aïeux,
> Que des palais Romains le front audacieux;
> Plus que le marbre dur me plaît l'ardoise fine,
>
> Plus mon Loire gaulois que le Tibre latin,
> Plus mon petit Liré que le mont Palatin,
> Et plus que l'air marin la douceur angevine.

The profile of my translation process may perhaps be most clearly demonstrated through an analysis of my various drafts. The actual translation procedure was obviously preceded by several readings of the original poem until I was sure that I had grasped the syntax and the various definitions of words that appeared to reflect Middle French usage (*saison*, *âge*, *usage*, *raison*, *audacieux*) and syntax that a hasty perusal might lead one to misinterpret ("Quand reverrai-je . . . de mon petit village / Fumer la cheminée . . . ?"). I then made a photocopy of the poem and started with a rather literal translation in the margins of that copy. At this stage and in subsequent revisions I must say that I actually "think aloud on paper." A French proverb avers that "thought is born in the mouth" (la pensée naît dans la bouche), and for me a corollary exists by which a translation's genesis may be found in its revisions. I repeatedly enter corrections and emendations in the text—sometimes using pencil or different ink colors—until the rough product is virtually illegible. Then, while I can still decipher this oft-retouched draft, I copy the latest version on the computer; and even at this stage I find myself reversing some choices or making additional changes, for the typed version provides new visual insights and verbal inspirations. There follows a series of revisions and printouts as I wrestle with the subtleties of rhythm and the technicalities of the rhyme and meter. The actual work of these many revisions takes place at various venues: on the computer or in writing when I am seated at my desk; in the evening or during the night in jottings made after I have gone to bed; or sometimes, during the final stages of the process, even in mental reflections when I am out walking, watching TV, or waiting for my car to be serviced. Two recent technical recall visits to replace airbags in my car may thus be considered of special significance!

The Du Bellay translation procedure varied slightly from this sequence. I was looking at a selection of poems by Du Bellay in an old textbook and I started to mull a rough translation of Sonnet XXXI of *Les Regrets*. I was in bed and didn't want to write in the actual book or get up to photocopy the text. Instead, I grabbed a piece of paper and started making a literal translation of the first part of the poem. I ended up spending an hour or two translating the octet of the sonnet and making lots of changes. I returned to this piece of paper over several days until it was almost indecipherable (Fig. 1, p. 97).

Although I was not terribly excited by what I had done so far, I decided to revert to my usual practice of annotating an actual text. I printed out some Du Bellay poems from the Internet[2] and then worked directly on that copy (Fig. 2, p. 98). This version of the entire poem returned some of the first draft's solutions to the drawing board for reconsideration and further brainstorming.

Subsequent vacillations and corrections were fewer and, perhaps, even more frustrating. After all, Du Bellay's syntax is straightforward and his poem's beauty lies in its gentle and unpretentious reminiscence of a quiet and better place. The emendations became fewer and fewer as the process tapered off, so

2. https://fr.wikisource.org/wiki/Les_Regrets_(Du_Bellay), accessed January 22, 2013.

to speak (Figs. 3–7, pp. 99–103), until I hit a wall before I reached my hoped-for destination. Here is the final—or more likely penultimate or even antepenultimate—draft of my translation of Sonnet XXXI:

Sonnet XXXI [Les Regrets]

Joachim Du Bellay

How fortunate is he who, like Ulysses
Or like Jason who sailed off to claim the Golden
    Fleece,
Returns, tested and wiser, from trips overseas
To live the rest of his life among kin in peace.

Alas, when shall I see my village again?
The smoke rising from my chimney? Which
    season shall find me
Once more back home in my old humble demesne
Whose garden is, to me, a province or a country?

I far prefer the dwelling my forebears called
    home
To all the pompous façades of the palaces in
    Rome;
And to hard marble slabs I prefer slates thin as
    wafers,

To the Latin Tiber my Gallic Loire valley,
To Palatine Hill my small town of Liré,
And to the sea breezes the soft Angevin zephyrs.

To reiterate, this chapter is intended to be a "familiar essay" about the rigors and hurdles involved in improving a formal verse translation and not a pretext to present a superlative transcreation in English. Events, times, fashions, and a translator's own personal aging and consequent esthetic maturation all change. The final emendation is never made, only a final compromise. As I mentioned above, my latest version of Sonnet XXXI may not be final. Even now, as I type the final draft of this book, I find myself wishing somehow to improve the music of the last line. I feel nagging doubts about the geographical adjective "Angevine" in English. How many readers will have ever heard this word or not be troubled by its pronunciation? They are much more likely to know or accept "Anjou's" in this closure. I have four alternate versions of that line begging to be considered: "And to a sea breeze Anjou's gentle zephyrs"; "And to sea breezes Anjou's gentle zephyrs"; "And to sea breezes soft Angevine zephyrs"; or "And to the sea breeze soft Angevine zephyrs." There are no doubt other possibilities, as well. And the extensive changes and restorations riddling my drafts of the second quatrain and the final tercet would suggest that there remain substantial possibilities for improvement in those stanzas, too. Indeed, the drafts and my own uncertainties reflected in them tend to support my claim—or reluctant admission—that no matter how interesting or personally rewarding this translation may have been as a process or creative journey it falls short of the initial expectations I had for recreation of a valid poem in English.

These days the trendy epistemological wisdom maintains that one can achieve success or learn more through failure than one can through success. Ah! Would that this were true!

5

Translating Baudelaire's "Les Plaintes d'un Icare" and Recalibrating the Scales

> Double, double, toil and trouble;
> Fire burn and cauldron bubble.
> —*Macbeth*, IV, 1

Au Lecteur: I have once again been amusing myself with the translation of an old chestnut, in this case Baudelaire's "Les Plaintes d'un Icare."

Once again, you may be asking yourself: "Who needs yet another translation of this poem?" To which I can only reply that no one needs it but that I find translation to be a highly creative way of interacting with a poem while creating a whole spectrum of new poems "all my own." On average, these formal poems take me through many drafts, each of which gives me the immediate joy of "writing a new poem" and the satisfaction of having improved on my earlier versions. And there is always the outside chance that such tender loving care will lead to a better result than is to be found in existing translations done by others, regardless of the translator's literary stature.

In this regard, the retranslation of a well-known poem will entail not a dialogue with the poet one is translating, but a virtual conference call with that poet and the translators who have already tried their hand at interpreting the original text. And, in turn, we are faced with the old question of who is the beneficiary of a successful translation. Usually one speaks of the benefit the original author reaps from the larger dissemination of his or her work and also the benefit to readers of the target language whose knowledge is broadened as a result of the availability of the translated author's message and art. I am submitting that an often-overlooked beneficiary of the translation is the translator. Ignoring for a moment the inherent importance or value of the original text transposed into another language as well as the literary and possibly financial benefit to both author and translator of the original text, we would do well to consider the personal creative benefit to the translator. In other words, one who undertakes a labor of love by translating once again an oft-translated but still challenging poem by, say, Rinaldo d'Aquino, Dante, Ronsard, Corneille, Baudelaire, Bo Carpelan, Tomas Tranströmer, Giacomo Leopardi, Giuseppe Ungaretti, or Mario Luzi may or may not succeed in creating a new self-sustaining poem in the "translator's language" even while "nailing" the general sense and esthetic thrust of the original. It is my contention that, win or lose, translation is an enlightening and fulfilling mental activity. Let me offer a homely analogy.

I inherited my father's devotion to solving crossword puzzles; but in my dotage, I have found that solving crossword puzzles is a less satisfying activity than working on new versions of selected short formal classic poems. I think I have figured out why. Both pastimes are good exercise for the mind, but when you have fully solved a crossword puzzle you have merely revealed a verbal structure or matrix that someone else has already fully formulated. In short, when you have completed the puzzle you have certainly discovered the puzzle author's creation buried in the document and its clues; and I suppose you have to a degree satisfied a deep-lying aesthetic appreciation for balance and symmetry in your sustained contemplation of the actual puzzle grid. On the other hand, when you create a successful equivalent formal verse translation in the target language, you have surely solved a problem, but you have also created a new and unique poetic structure of your own devising. This process is much more satisfying! And if the translation just fails or peters out here and there, you can always discard it, much as you might abandon a boringly easy or overly difficult crossword puzzle when it no longer proves to be amusing.

Below is the fifteenth draft of my English version of "Les Plaintes d'un Icare"! I'll let it sit for a few months and maybe then revisit it again. Or, perhaps not. Anyway, I suggest that one read this translation aloud in a plain and somewhat prosy manner so that the run-ons (*enjambements*) and rhymes fall in their appointed subordinate places. . . . That is the effect I was trying to achieve. If you don't feel like reading it through nor care to make the effort to savor some of its verbal effects, just trash it as you would a crossword puzzle that is either too easy or too hard to hold your interest!

An Icarian Lament

Charles Baudelaire

The pleasure seekers who merely make love
To whores are sated and quite content;
But my arms are broken, for I was intent
On embracing the clouds that billowed above.

It is thanks to the stars, rivaled by none,
Flaming in the sky's remote infinity,
That my wasted eyes now only can see
Imagined versions of the sun.

I tried in vain to reach the rings
Of space's edge or its middle sky;
Under I know not what fiery eye,
I can feel the melting of my wings;

And burnt by my lust for a beauty sublime,
I can't even imagine that one day a sea

Might bear my name as its honoree
And serve as my tomb for the rest of time.

I seldom solicit or receive advice from the friends to whom I sometimes send drafts of my formal translations. The few suggestions that I do receive usually reflect that person's poetic style and I only tend to consider their suggestions when these actually improve the poem. Often the comments touch on a word or rhythmic effect that I had already labored over and revised without complete satisfaction. This particular translation of Baudelaire's "Les Plaintes d'un Icare" is a good case in point.

Two friends to whom I sent an early draft were Catharine Savage Brosman and Hédi Abdel-Jaouad who made suggestions concerning the first stanza. The translation was improved by a single word suggested by Cathy. In an early draft I had written "The paramours who always make love . . ." I felt that "paramours" was too lofty and too emotionally reciprocal for the type of sex workers Baudelaire wrote about and I subsequently changed that line to "The pleasure seekers who always make love." I was uncomfortable with "always" because it suggests a lofty status for the whores but I repeatedly let it slip by through many revisions. Cathy, with her sharp eye for detail, zeroed in on this bothersome word and suggested "merely." Perfect! I immediately made this small but excellent emendation.

Another word I had used in earlier versions and had finally discarded was the last word in the third line: "bent." I had dropped that word in favor of "intent." I subsequently wavered in the fourth line between "towered" and "billowed" as a modifier for "clouds" in line 4 and finally opted for the latter, after which I never went back to considering "bent / on" rather than "intent / on." It is not surprising perhaps that Hédi Abdel-Jaouad—without knowing that I had already agonized over the word—wondered why I didn't use "bent" instead of "intent," rightly suggesting that "bent" would add to the alliteration while keeping the rhyme. Now, I had read these lines aloud over and over again and my reservations were visceral, so to speak. My response to Hédi was perhaps uncouth, but then again at times so are Baudelaire's poems. I detailed my struggles with the passage in question, explaining that one problem with "bent" is that the word brings with it semantic echoes of that word in British English (crooked, dishonest). However, I admitted that the lure of alliteration persuaded me to abandon "towering" in favor of "that billowed." Once the latter change was made, the alliteration seemed to me excessive: " . . . *broken, for I was bent / On embracing the clouds that billowed above.*" After I read these lines aloud, I was unable to dissociate them from a near-forgotten joke I had heard in the 1950s:

> A traveling salesman checked in at his hotel after a hard day's work and was enjoying a deep and

> luxurious bubble bath. He had rung for room service and when the hotel waiter came to his room the salesman called out to inform him that he was in the tub and that the waiter should come to the bathroom door to take the order. The salesman asked for a ham on rye sandwich and the waiter left to fill the order.
>
> The waiter returned in due course with a tray-stand bearing a sandwich and a bottle of beer. The salesman in the bathtub exclaimed: "That sandwich looks great, but I didn't ask for a beer." The waiter looked confused and replied: "As I was leaving to get you your sandwich, I could have sworn I heard you mutter: 'And bring me a bottle of Budweiser, Buddy!'"

A witches' brew indeed, "Double, double, toil and trouble; / Fire burn and cauldron bubble." Having recalled this cretinous joke from my college years, I was no longer able to countenance using the word "bent" rather than "intent" in my translation.

This anecdote serves additionally to remind us that a literary translator is never free of personal input and emotions that might color his or her version of a source text.

6

"Free Verse"; Free of What?

> If we are going to follow this modern way of free verse—free from music, free from meter, free from . . . well, they even write bad prose and call it poetry—then our ear will be ruined.
>
> —Husnī Farīz

> So you can translate the modern poetry into any other language easily, but you cannot translate the classical. Modern poetry is not a luxury!
>
> —Mahmoud Haider

Will you think it absurd if I say that in some ages and cultures formal poetry has been defended as a matter of national interest, like vital mineral, water, or oil reserves? Or that Formalists might view Free-Verse Practitioners as nothing short of insurgents or saboteurs? Well, read on!

In 1983, during a USIA-sponsored lecture and poetry-reading tour of the Near East and the Maghreb, I repeatedly came across an interesting variation of the literary generation gap, one that was perhaps to be expected given the nature of the Arabic language and the strong poetic tradition that has for millennia been placed squarely on the shoulders of storytellers and poets in that culture.

The Arabic language is complex but algorithmic and logical in its syntactic-semantic permutations. For example, prefixes, suffixes, and vowel changes often signal the function of words built on consonantal roots like K-T-B (a cluster that denotes the act of writing) as in *kataba* (he wrote), *kitāb* (book) *kātib* (writer), *maktab* (desk, office), *maktabat* (library, bookstore), *maktūb* (that which is written, whence kismet or fate). Augmentatives generally display a predictable pronunciation and stress shift based on the consonants used in the adjective: *kabīr* (big) yields *akbaru* (bigger, older), *djamīl* (beautiful) yields *adjmalu* (more beautiful), *samīn* (fat) yields *asmanu* (fatter), and so on. It is not amazing, then, that the language should foster—or perhaps reflect—a very strong cognitive sense of rhythmic predictability related to the semantics; and spawn an inherent appreciation of and respect for metrical conventions. The stronger the convention, the more difficult it is to embrace linguistic and literary experimentation, such as free verse and texts that depend for esthetic effect on the dazzling use of the image.

It should come as no surprise, for example, that France with its strong tradition of metrical laws based on a regular inviolable syllable count had to wait until the 1880s for free verse to be tolerated, while American metrics—based on the much looser English "foot" system whose parameters governing poetic license authorize a variable syllabic count in each measure or foot and acknowledge a liberal policy regarding the occasional substitution of individual metrical feet, such as a dactyl for an iamb, in a line—permitted Walt Whitman and other trailblazers to abandon metrics altogether at a much earlier date. Even Charles Baudelaire, inspired by the precursor Aloysius Bertrand, turned directly to the prose poem to unfetter his muse, a departure far less daring at the time than the smallest violation of the iron-clad tradition of metrical formalism that would not tolerate a metrical blunder or "faux vers" such as an eleven- or thirteen-syllable alexandrine.

At the beginning of my USIA tour, in the Q&A period following a talk I gave at Yarmouk University in Irbid, Jordan, a student objected to my labeling as "poetry" short pieces by Robert Bly, James Wright, and other contemporary American poets. He felt that the texts were pleasant enough but that they did not constitute poetry, being nothing more than images and far too brief. Poetry should, he maintained, have a degree of heft, structure, and repetition or it is simply not poetry.

After this little contretemps, I realized that it would be wise in other upcoming recitals and lectures to be proactive and to explain the rationale behind the dynamics of contemporary American poetics at the beginning of my presentation and to include in my readings at least several poems graced by structured stanzas, refrains, rhymes, and the like.

As my tour moved on through Jordon and Egypt and then on to Algeria and Morocco, this debate as to whether or not there can be poetry free of form recurred and tended to pit older established authors against younger writers. The older authors equated structure in the poetry to the very existence of their intellectual and artistic patrimony. To threaten form in poetry was tantamount to threatening society and culture itself.

In Amman, my USIA-arranged activities included a meeting with the Jordanian poets Husnī Farīz, who was in his mid-seventies, and Mahmoud Haider, who was about forty. During this trip I was also gathering material for an article I was writing for *World Literature Today* about the local literary scene in the several countries I was visiting and Mahmoud Haider and Husnī Farīz heartily agreed to our discussion being recorded, with the understanding I would be publishing all or parts of the transcript in my *WLT* article.[1]

I brought up the question of avant-garde experimental writing. Although they expressed mutual

1. Shortly after my return to the United States the two epigraphs at the head of this chapter and the longer extract below were published in my chronicle: "Letter from the Near East and the Maghreb," *World Literature Today* 57, no. 1 (Winter 1983): 55–58.

respect and admiration, the two poets clearly disagreed on the value of "modern" techniques such as free verse. Below is a pertinent excerpt of our discussion.

> FARĪZ: The point is, you [American and Western writers] have so many kinds of art: sculpture, music, painting and poetry; and if you lose poetry, you don't lose a great deal. But our poetry is the only thing for which we are famous in the world, and Arab lyric poetry is the first in the world. If we are going to follow this modern way of free verse (free from music, free from meter, free from . . . well, they even write bad prose and call it poetry), then our ear will be ruined.
>
> SELLIN: My Arabic professor liked to say that the earliest Arabs, being nomadic, could not take museums and libraries with them and therefore poured all their genius into the language. If that is true, wouldn't the loss of your language be, in a sense, the loss of your libraries and museums?
>
> FARĪZ: Poetry to us is not luxury; it is daily bread. We want to fight for our lives, or we will be exterminated. It has been determined that we shall be exterminated, and if we lose the communication of language, what else will remain? Our language is our life, whether it is colloquial or classical.
>
> HAIDER: The younger people write the modern way. There is a relation between the age and the way you write. Mr. Husnī Farīz insists on

writing in the classical way. I can write—every poet can write—in the classical way or he is not a poet, really, because those are the roots of Arabic poetry; but the younger people try to reach every modern mentality. The ages of space and the ages of civilization are different now, so we try to reach the young mentalities. The subjects now are different. The old poet used to stand in the ruins and describe them. The modern poet doesn't do this but writes about human, political and social problems. So you can translate the modern poetry into any other language easily, but you cannot translate the classical. Modern poetry is not a luxury!

SELLIN: You have both spoken of poetry—classical and modern, respectively—as not being a luxury. You, Mr. Mahmoud Haider, have spoken of the political authenticity of modern poetry, and you, Mr. Husnī Farīz, of maintaining one's identity by maintaining traditional meters. This is a form of militancy, isn't it? I wonder if the experimental poet—breaking with tradition—feels that his work has any urgency in a time of political concern. In America, during times of political disenchantment—such as during the Vietnam War—poets have sometimes stopped writing as a form of protest or have at least felt that their esthetic works lacked relevance.

FARĪZ: We write poetry protesting against such events taking place in the Arab world. If our

> government or state is antagonistic to some problem, and it is not just, we will attack it—even if we do not publish [the protest], for we are not free to say everything. We protest factual things.

It is interesting that later during my trip, at a convivial evening with writers in Rabat, Ahmed Sefrioui—the Moroccan writer whose prose works *La boîte à merveille* and *Le chapelet d'ambre* place him among the leading Francophone Maghrebian writers in the 1950s—expressed esthetic ideas in terms almost identical to those I had heard in Jordan. Sefrioui equated the rejection of rhyme and meter and traditional rhetorical devices and tropes to an attack on the overall heritage of his country and his people: "Our poetry is our patrimony. It takes the place of museums and libraries. If the young poet destroys our poetic tradition, he not only destroys the poems but also rejects our whole artistic patrimony." After Sefrioui had left, one writer took me aside and said: "Out of respect for Sefrioui's reputation and his contribution to Moroccan literature no one spoke out, but many of us younger poets feel quite the contrary about free verse."

Thus it would appear that in the Arab world the abandonment by younger poets of the poetic formalism revered by their elders is not simply a case of the ongoing rolling alienation that occurs between generations, but rather a major esthetic and cultural shift involving a veritable identity crisis. One wonders if poets should seek universal insights afforded by international trends in art or remain faithful to the integrated values inherent in their ethos? Or, might not the poet, as Mahmoud Haider implied, rather prefer to pursue either one or both of these paths in an effort to reach a wider and more relevant readership?

7

Baudelaire's "The Enemy"—Tracking the Revisions

Ma jeunesse ne fut qu'un ténébreux orage,
Traversé çà et là par de brillants soleils;
Le tonnerre et la pluie ont fait un tel ravage,
Qu'il reste en mon jardin bien peu de fruits
vermeils.

Voilà que j'ai touché l'automne des idées,
Et qu'il faut employer la pelle et les râteaux
Pour rassembler à neuf les terres inondées,
Où l'eau creuse des trous grands comme des
tombeaux.

Et qui sait si les fleurs nouvelles que je rêve
Trouveront dans ce sol lavé comme une grève
Le mystique aliment qui ferait leur vigueur?

—Ô douleur! Ô douleur! Le temps mange la vie,
Et l'obscur Ennemi qui nous ronge le coeur
Du sang que nous perdons croît et se fortifie!

I composed and translated verse for many years without giving much thought to the process I was undergoing. I enjoyed hearing and discussing anecdotes and quips about the creative process, like Archibald MacLeish's dictum that "a poem should not mean / but be," but I have only recently become interested in the meanderings, setbacks, and breakouts that one experiences during the intense engagement of recreating in one language a complex poetic work composed in another language.

The essays in *The Magic Mirror* are an intimate exploration of the dynamics of poetic translation, but I also thought it worthwhile to take a cold objective look at the vagaries of the actual emendations threaded through some of the drafts of the revisions in the translation of one brief poem, in this instance Baudelaire's sonnet "L'Ennemi."

Below one will find a selection of seven of the many drafts that I scribbled of this translation. A perusal and an analysis of the changes highlighted in bold type in these drafts will trace the impetus or trajectory of the typical revision process that blazes its trail through the murky woods toward the clearing of a viable rendition. Cynics will suggest that it might have made more economic sense to have summarized the changes and not reproduce these facsimiles, but I find it interesting to actually relive the critical moments of excitement, hard work, and self-doubt that left their own distinct heart line, so to speak. I was not quite aware of the relative arrhythmia in the versions and the desperate efforts at defibrillation that were going on until I examined a printout of the lifeline.

The most apparent phenomena of interest in a scan of these drafts appear in the first three drafts, in the shift in metrical conventions in the fourth draft, and in the rather trivial vacillations that reverberate in the last three drafts as a result of my having resurrected or rejected earlier revisions of a word or two. The initial acceptable draft was a result of many pages of scribbled experimentation involving vocabulary, rhyme, and meter options. I would define that stage as composition of the translation. There then followed the arduous process of rewriting or revision and the wrestling match with the various opportunities that the translingual and transcultural process offered as I tried to pin down an inevitable-sounding version of Baudelaire's poem. This struggle is most evident in the major changes made in the second draft in which such things as fidelity to the feel and content of the original have held considerable sway and in which we might sense a certain unease with details that have a tinny ring in modern English, such as the rhyme-induced inversion in the seventh line: "To recover anew those lands with flood waters fraught."

The next major rewriting of the translation occurred after the third draft presented here at a moment when I had hit a wall and thought of abandoning the translation. The transcreation involved in rendering a French metrical piece into the more elastic English metrics provided an escape route around the wall with, of course, no guarantee of improvement or ultimate success. In opting for iambic tetrameter rather than pentameter I could still add weak syllables and substitute feet and I found myself more in control of the musicality of the English version without having to torture the semantics to achieve a consistent metrical structure. The third and fourth drafts required a different set of esthetic considerations and are technically parsed and sometimes recited differently even if the actual structures appear rather similar to the casual eye.

After that crucial shift in metrical line makeup, the rest of the drafts entailed repeated readings aloud of those lines and words that seemed to need tweaking. The shift in metrics even made a few images and words that I had found unacceptable in the earliest versions now quite viable as I fine-tuned the translations' musicality.

Translation is a bit like stud poker. Each revision and ultimately every substitute word is a gamble, but one that no bluff can mediate. In trying to fill a straight flush hand for a winner, the fifth card one opts for may be a high ace of spades that yet leaves you with a complete bust or it may be a lowly deuce of clubs or trey of diamonds that leaves you with an unexpected winner.

I make no claim that "The Enemy" is a brilliant translation and I may even one day revisit the latest version with an eye to improving it. I offer it here simply as a scan and analysis of the transcreative gambling process that goes on in the mind and soul of a translator, that process being especially complicated and interesting when the translation is of verse in rhyme and meter.

The Translation Revision Process (July 10–August 28, 2014)

First Draft of Translation, July 10, 2014

The Enemy

Charles Baudelaire

My youth was nothing but a stormy sky,
Pierced here and there by brilliant shafts of light;
Ruinous thunder and rain are the reasons why
There now remain in my garden few fruits that
 are bright.

Now that I find myself in the Autumn of thought
When one has to make use of shovels and rakes
To recover anew those lands with flood waters
 fraught,
Where water scoops out holes as big as graves.

And who knows if the new flowers that I find
 myself dreaming
Shall in this soil hard as the strand in an ebb
 tide's streaming
Find the mystical nourishment needed to make
 them into art.

Oh Grief! the grief! For time is consuming our lives,
And the faint dark Enemy who is gnawing at our heart,
Fortified by the blood we are shedding, just grows and thrives.

Second Draft of Translation, July 12, 2014

My youth was nothing **more than one long storm,**
Pierced **now and then** by **sunny** shafts of light;
Ruinous thunder and **pelting** rain **were the norm**
And the reason my garden now has few fruits that are bright.

Now **I am in** the Autumn **days of life's** thought
When one **resorts to using rakes and spades**
To **restore** anew those lands **where flood waters have wrought**
Deep ruts and dug holes as large as graves.

And who knows if the new flowers that I find myself dreaming
Shall in this soil **packed like a beach by the** ebb tide's streaming
Yet find that arcane nourishment that turns them into art.

Alas! Alas! Time is consuming our lives;
And the **obscure** Enemy **‹›** gnawing away at our heart— [‹› delete **who is**]

Fortified by the blood we are shedding—takes root and thrives.

Third Draft of Translation, July 14, 2014, a.m.

My youth was nothing but **a long dark** storm,
Pierced **here and there** by sunny shafts of light;
Ruinous thunderbolts and pelting rain were the norm
And the reason my garden now **bears** few **blossoms** that are bright.

I find myself now in the **Autumn of life's** realm of thought,
When one resorts to using rakes and spades
To restore **‹›** those lands where **the** flood waters have wrought [‹› delete **anew**]
Deep ruts and **gouged out** holes as large as graves.

And who knows if the new flowers that I find myself dreaming,
In this soil packed **hard** like a beach **in an** ebb tide's streaming,
Shall yet find **the** arcane **nourishment to morph** into art.

Alas! Alas! Time **goes on** consuming our lives;
And the obscure Enemy gnawing away at our heart—
Fortified by the blood we are **losing**—takes root and thrives.

At this point I decided that tetrameter might work better than pentameter in a successful rendering of this poem.

Fourth Draft of Translation, July 14, 2014, p.m.

My youth was ‹› but a long dark storm, [‹› delete **nothing**]
Pierced here and there by shafts of light;
Ruinous thunderbolts and ‹› rain were the norm [‹› delete **pelting**]
And the reason my garden ‹› bears few **blooms** that are bright. [‹› delete **now**]

‹› Now in the Autumn of life's span of thought, [‹› delete **I find myself**]
I have to resort to rakes and spades
To restore those lands where ‹› flood waters have wrought [‹› delete **the**]
Long ruts and holes as **deep** as graves.

And who knows if ‹› new flowers that I find myself dreaming, [‹› delete **the**]
In soil like sand in an ebb tide's streaming,
Shall find the nourishment to grow into art.

Sadly, Time goes on consuming our lives;
And the obscure Enemy gnawing away at our heart,
Fortified by the blood we are losing, ‹› thrives. [‹› delete **just**]

Fifth Draft of Translation, August 27, 2014

My youth was but a long dark storm,
Pierced here and there by shafts of light;
Ruinous thunderbolts **and downpours** the norm
And the reason **the blooms in my garden aren't bright**.

Now in the autumn of life's span of thought,
I have to resort to rakes and spades
To restore those lands where flood waters have wrought
Long ruts and holes as deep as graves.

And who knows if new flowers that I find myself dreaming,
In soil like sand in an ebb tide's streaming,
Shall find the nourishment to **mature** into art.

Sadly, Time goes on consuming our lives;
And the obscure Enemy gnawing away at our heart,
Strengthened by the blood we are losing, **just** thrives.

Sixth Draft of Translation, August 28, 2014

My youth was but a long dark storm,
Pierced here and there by shafts of light;
Ruinous thunderbolts and downpours the norm

And the reason the blooms in my garden aren't
bright.

Now in the autumn of life's span of thought,
I have to resort to rakes and spades
To restore those lands where flood waters have
wrought
Long ruts and holes as deep as graves.

And who knows if new flowers that I find myself
dreaming,
In soil like sand in an ebb tide's streaming,
Shall find the nourishment to **grow** into art.

Sadly, Time goes on consuming our lives;
And the obscure Enemy gnawing away at our
heart,
Fortified by the blood we are losing, thrives.

Seventh and Latest Draft of Translation, August 28, 2014

The Enemy

Charles Baudelaire

My youth was **nothing** but a long dark storm,
Pierced here and there by shafts of light;
Wild thunderbolts and downpours were the
norm

And the reason the plants in my garden aren't
bright.

Now in the autumn of life's span of thought,
I've had to resort to rakes and spades
To restore those lands where flood waters have
wrought
Long ruts and holes as deep as graves.

And who knows if new flowers that I find myself
dreaming,
In soil like sand in the ebb tide's streaming,
Shall find the nourishment to **mature** into art.

Sadly, time goes on consuming our lives;
And the obscure Enemy gnawing away at our
heart,
Strengthened by the blood we are losing, thrives.

8

Challenges and Rewards

The Dynamics of Co-Translation

> A successful literary translation melds two esthetic souls, that of the author and that of the translator, into a third soul that brings the final translated text to life.

Ideally the translator of a poem will know the original author's language and culture and have personal access to that author for clarification of obscure references and ambiguities, as well as to discuss the translator's own rationale for noticeable departures from the structure and semantics of the original. However, many literary translations are done by two or more translators, usually one who knows the source language and culture well and the other who has mastery over the target language and its cultural nuances, including such things as the use of rhyme and meter.

Co-translation has recently emerged as a viable separate subcategory in Translation Studies and the dynamics of the co-translation process involves a number of permutations and vectors. It also involves many thorny challenges that seemed to be ignored or negotiable in the early years of the twentieth century when many writers became expatriates and lived abroad for extended periods of time. Those halcyon days were abruptly curtailed during the rise of fascism and the advent of World War II.

In the first two decades after World War II, the surging interest in global transculturalism outstripped the foreign-language acumen of most emerging American poets; and to embrace the contemporary poetry in other cultures through translation they found it necessary to ask someone familiar with the original language to make a literal word-for-word conversion of a poem, often into something resembling pidgin English, that they would work over to make into a viable poem. In such an instance the magic mirror may prove more akin to a fun-house mirror. The final poet/translator is actually interacting with the first "hack" translator in such a way that the result is hit or miss: by some miracle the resulting text may come out as a genuine transcreation, but it is more likely to be an elongated or bloated amusement-park mirror reflection of the final poet-translator, perhaps with a faint image of the distorted hack beside him or her in the photo booth holding V-sign rabbit ears above the poet's head.

I have heard tell of cases in which the translation of a text in collaboration with its author or with a qualified linguist has proven frustrating, to say the least, and has even led to an abrupt end to the collaboration and, more than likely, to a friendship. Normally the author of the original text is a valuable resource, especially if he or she doesn't know the target language well and therefore relies on the translator's judgment in conveying matters of style and content in the target language. Over the years I have usually worked alone with an occasional clarification from the author if that person is alive and willing. I have found that authors are usually pleased, even thrilled, to have their work published in another language. I have, with their cooperation, translated dozens of poets, among them Léopold Sédar Senghor, who graciously provided me with a personal glossary of some references to African things, people, and places in one of his long poems, and Tomas Tranströmer, who fortunately noticed and laughed heartily at an embarrassing howler in one of my drafts where in my haste I had misread *kisa* (to squint) as *kissa* (to pee)! What with the unexpected "torque" in the linkages in some of Tranströmer's imagery, that line in my draft had seemed odd, but not utterly off the Tranströmer radar screen!

From the early 1950s to today, I have translated poetry alone or with minimal advice from a colleague or from the author of the source text. It has been an interesting journey with some unexpected side trips. The interaction with living authors proved especially interesting. Most poets were pleased that their work was thus appreciated; and some reciprocated and translated into their language poems I had written in English. One especially gratifying result of such co-operation and genuine friendship was the itinerary that ultimately led me to compose original poems directly in French. I started by solving unresolvable snags in cultural equivalency or language incompatibility in order to "salvage" a French poet's translation by suggesting a rephrasing of an entire section directly in French with an eye to skirting the issue entirely. I gradually gained enough confidence to move on to writing poems directly in French, especially during the years I spent immersed in a French-speaking environment.

My negotiation with poets whose work I translated into English was usually a pleasant and edifying experience that in many cases led to long-lasting friendships. The dynamics of translation involved complex strategies and personal preferences that took various turns. In working with foreign-language poets, I found some individuals to be headstrong and difficult to deal with while others were generous and non-intrusive. I was—as a "transcreative" translator and a poet who was, himself, occasionally translated by other poets—presumably viewed by my counterparts through a similar kaleidoscope of emotions. Perhaps it was the capriciousness of dealing with living writers that led me, for many decades, generally to prefer to translate Early Modern, Romantic, and Post-Romantic verse and to somehow commune with those long-gone souls whom I came to understand and even cherish.

When it comes to a literary translation by a single translator, of the sort I have discussed in the preceding chapters, an acceptable result assumes a level of competence on the part of the translator, for a successful literary translation melds two esthetic souls, that of the author and that of the translator, into a third soul that brings the final translated text to life. By adding one or more other collaborators, one risks either eclipsing one or both of these two souls or else bringing in additional and perhaps excessive soul-power, so to speak.

Only two or three times did I have a problem with excessive input from an author whose work I had translated. However, the positive memories of my interaction with many foreign poets on three continents far outweigh the memories of those few irksome interactions. Suffice it to say, here, that I had never engaged in co-translation in the true sense of the word until recently, after I retired from my teaching career.

Now, after sixty years of translating poetry solo from several languages—albeit sometimes with attendant negotiations and useful consultation with authors and other translators—I recently found myself working with a third party on joint translation projects from Arabic poetry and from French prose. This collaborative work was necessary, on the one hand because of my limited Arabic and on the other because I have never taken a great interest in translating prose. But let me start at the beginning of this adventure in collaboration, one that has for me been as pleasant and productive as the several above-mentioned misadventures with headstrong poets or third-party advisors had been unsatisfactory and frustrating.

Between 1968 and 1991, I spent a total of two years in Arabic countries, primarily Algeria and Morocco; but my knowledge of French, a lack of foresight on my part, and the nature of the dialects spoken in the Maghreb prevented me from taking full advantage of these opportunities for linguistic immersion. Upon returning to the United States in 1969, I belatedly took a year or two of Arabic before other obligations forced me to abandon my study of that language. The result is that I studied Arabic on and off for almost fifty years, but it has been a matter of taking the first two years over and over again as refresher classes so that I wouldn't completely forfeit the time and effort already invested in the study of the language. Thus, I have a rudimentary knowledge of Arabic and can read uncomplicated texts with a dictionary. My speaking and oral comprehension competencies are not very good. I truly regret having failed to profit from the years I taught and traveled in the Maghreb, Egypt, and Jordan when I could have gained some fluency in Modern Standard Arabic and its dialects.

The upshot of all this is that it never occurred to me to attempt a translation of poetry from the

Arabic, although I have written a few haiku-like poems directly in Arabic. I might be able to decipher the content of a short poem, but I wouldn't have the ear to tell a melodious poem from a tinny one or to acknowledge the power of a poem's tropes, images, or nuanced evocations of cultural poetic conventions like the *waṣf*. Circumstances led to my involvement in the translation of poems from Arabic and my first real and willing experience of translating literary material with a co-translator. The best way to explain how this collaboration came about and how the co-translator and I worked together is, perhaps, to describe events leading up to the collaboration.

The last time I sat in on beginning and intermediate classes at the University of Pennsylvania in order to try once again to refresh my stale Arabic, my instructor was a Moroccan named Mbarek Sryfi. We became friends and met periodically for lunch to talk about language and literature. Sryfi asked me if I would be interested in translating with him *Les Arabes et l'art du récit: Une étrange familiarité* by the Moroccan critic and scholar Abdelfattah Kilito. I told him that I was not particularly interested in translating prose, preferring to translate poetry.

We then worked together translating some Arabic-language poems by Moroccans Hassan Najmi, Aïcha Bassry, Ouidad Benmoussa, and Malika al-Assimi. Our modus operandi for rendering these straightforward free verse poems was quite simple. Mbarek made rough translations of the poems which he then gave to me along with the Arabic originals. I read the originals as well as I could, using Hans Wehr's *A Dictionary of Modern Written Arabic* and cross-referencing vocabulary options in *The Concise Oxford English-Arabic Dictionary*; and then I corrected sentences and rephrased passages of Mbarek's English drafts, noting those passages in which the meaning of his English version escaped me or when I didn't understand the original well enough to know who or what was the proper antecedent. Our bête noire was the pesky *iḍāfa* (إضافة), a genitive construction in Arabic in which it is often difficult to detect that which is possessed and who or what is the possessor. The *iḍāfa* often contains an ambiguity that can remain inoffensively ambiguous in the original Arabic but must be clarified in an English translation. It is not unlike one's possibly using the wrong antecedent in parsing meticulously in English a clause like "the collection of poems he loves the most." Is it the poems or the collection that he loves the most? Or when translating a French sentence like "La femme du curé a transmis ses meilleurs vœux aux visiteurs," do we here translate "*ses*" as "his best wishes" (the pastor's) or "her best wishes" (the wife's)? In translating the French sentence, the translator has only two options: to choose one or the other of these options ("his" or "her") or to revise the passage radically in order to skirt the ambiguity by other means. The periodic work sessions during which Mbarek and I conferred and ironed out snags, connotations, and the like were interesting, instructive, and enjoyable. We published a number of these co-translated poems in *Metamorphoses*, *World Literature Today*, and *CELAAN Review*.

One day, while we were working on these poems, Mbarek Sryfi handed me some pages of prose he had translated from Abdelfattah Kilito's *Les Arabes et l'art du récit: Une étrange familiarité* and asked me to take a quick look at them. Well, after having worked with Mbarek and since the original was in French I felt comfortable enough making rather thorough corrections and stylistic revisions in his extract. He then urged me once again to join him in co-translating this book. My knowledge of the original language was not an issue. I had no need for a collaborator and could have translated the book on my own. But since we were continuing to collaborate on the Arabic poetry, I finally reminded Mbarek that I rarely translated prose but that I had, as a teacher and as an editor of several scholarly journals, spent forty-five years correcting other people's prose in both French and English.

We agreed that we would proceed much as we had in translating the poetry, namely that he would make a rough preliminary translation of Kilito's essays, and I would then make corrections and where necessary rewrite the English draft to ensure fluidity and idiomatic consistency. These drafts were exchanged and discussed many times before being finalized. *Arabs and the Art of Storytelling: A Strange Familiarity* was published in a handsome edition by Syracuse University Press in December 2014 and was a finalist in nonfiction for the 28th French-American Foundation and Florence Gould Foundation Translation Prize in 2015.

Mbarek deserved his listing as the lead translator in the collaboration because of his industry in making and coordinating the rough draft of the translation and in spurring the project along and in finding and dealing with the eventual publisher. My role primarily involved rewriting some of the material, polishing the grammar, revising the style here and there, and doing much of the spade work involved in preparing and proofreading the academic critical apparatus.

Our modus operandi was laborious and the translation of the rather brief Kilito book took almost two years from the moment Mbarek gave me that first extract until publication. But the process involved many fine work sessions lasting two or three hours, a good part of each session being devoted to discussions of grammar, digressions on literature, and idle personal conversation. I owe to Mbarek's persistence many hours of useful and purposeful and satisfying activity with which I could fill the post-retirement vacuum or doldrums that I have described in the introduction to these essays. I don't recall the precise chronology, but I believe it was shortly after we began our frequent translating sessions of the Arabic poems that

I turned to revising my own old unpublished poems and translations and once again became engrossed in translating classic verse poems such as the ones by Baudelaire, Du Bellay, Ronsard, and Verhaeren discussed in the preceding essays.

Conclusion

Conflict Resolution and the Quest for Inevitability

> Poetry pulses in the tension between the secure refuge of form and the lure of perilously unfettered verbal liberation.

In my first essay, I mention the "inevitability" of a good translation: "It now is obvious to me that the 'unease' I felt years ago after first translating the poem [Verhaeren's 'Le Navire'] was due to my failure to maintain, in the second and third stanzas, the sense of *inevitability* that marks virtually every good translation." I also notice that I refer several times in these essays to difficulties in sustaining a good translation when tackling the second stanza, even noting that in some of the original poems there is a decline in quality in the second or third stanza.

I was largely left to my own devices when I wrote my doctor's dissertation, but a few things I learned in the process proved to be of great value later on. I had always been an impetuous "flair" writer who would work feverishly during the eleventh hour to finish poems or term papers on time, depending on an interesting slant or on creative linkages, and sometimes, of course, on the requisite twelve-pack to sustain my own interest during the process and make the whole Augean academic process tolerable and, I hoped, help me produce writing that would pique the interest and appreciation of the professor or reader.

The year-long process of writing a book-length manuscript taught me to work from an outline and to return to my project on a more logical writing schedule that was not contingent on having drunk sufficient beer or harboring a genuine enthusiasm for the topic. I learned that it was far better to find a problem whose solution was challenging and interesting than to select an author one genuinely admired. In my case I was not particularly interested in Antonin Artaud as a person, but the challenge of unearthing from his oblique essays and incoherent albeit ecstatic ranting some sort of structured theoretical apparatus on dramatic art presented me with major esthetic and intellectual hurdles. Indeed, though cited regularly in the cultural press in the early 1960s for promoting a "Theater of Cruelty," Artaud had only been the subject of two books, both involving primarily his mental condition and his medical treatment. Thus I did learn how to sustain an academic study over extended time. I must say that, although my dissertation was published by the University of Chicago

Press and received favorable reviews, the whole process of qualifying for the PhD was a rocky road for me and, once capped and gowned, I swore that the next book I wrote would be one that I would enjoy writing. Indeed, my next book, *The Inner Game of Soccer* (Mountain View, CA: Anderson-World, 1976) was about officiating soccer.

One other structural lesson I learned from the dissertation process was one that I only came to appreciate many years later after the graduate school paranoia wore off. When I finally began my feverish eleventh-hour composition of the dissertation (an eleventh hour that was to last eleven months), I first composed more than a hundred pages of writing that I felt was nothing short of incandescent. I delivered that first section to my supervisor (Professor Robert K. Bishop of the University of Pennsylvania) and waited impatiently for the phone call that would surely announce that he had found my submission extraordinary. After a couple of weeks, I finally telephoned him and nervously asked him if he had found the time to read my material yet. His answer: "There are grave problems; come by my house and we can discuss them." When I got to his place, he said that perhaps seven pages of the more than a hundred pages I had given him might be salvageable but that the rest would have to be scrapped. He maintained that they were digressions irrelevant to my thesis!

I was devastated, but I took the deleted material and was quickly able to publish most of it in several journal articles and thought: "So there!" For example, one of the deleted digressions concerning the impact of Orientalism on several Western playwrights and touching on Artaud, Yeats, O'Neill, and half a dozen other dramatists was immediately accepted for publication by *France-Asie.*[1] It was only many years later that I would be ready to acknowledge that the excised material may have been of some value per se but had, indeed, consisted of a series of tangents.

On the level of stylistic micromanagement, I have over the years retained and even repeated to students three of my supervisor's suggestions, namely that in a dissertation one should "avoid literary pyrotechnics," "make one's style academic and dull as dishwater," and strive to achieve a feeling of "inevitability" in the discourse.

Recently, upon reading Paul Fussell's elegantly irreverent book *Poetic Meter and Poetic Form*, I was reminded of two of the elements discussed in these essays: the notions of "inevitability" and the creative sophomore jinx a poet or translator may experience in maintaining poetic thrust after a very successful opening stanza.

Fussell dwells nicely on the jinx involved in sustaining one's magisterial élan in the second quatrain or in making the successful transition from octet to

1. "The Oriental Influence in Modern Western Drama," *France-Asie* 21, no. 187 (Automne 1966): 85–92.

sestet in a Petrarchan sonnet: "There is always the temptation in the second quatrain merely to repeat or to reproject the matter of the first instead of advancing or really complicating the argument, description, or emotion. . . . It is the second quatrain that poses a challenge to every poet's capacity for genuine—rather than merely apparent—thematic development."[2]

Fussell also reinforces the notion of inevitability. He initially suggests an "axiom of economy and coherence" of poetic composition in which the "meter of a poem, no matter how extrinsically discovered and traditionally exploited by the poet, should give the illusion of having arisen intrinsically and subtly from within the uniqueness of the poetic occasion. . . . A master is one whose practice persuades us that his general metrical choice is the only thinkable one for his poem" (90–91).

A few pages later Fussell returns to this axiom to deduce a second critical principle that "substitutions for regular mechanically beautiful metrical cadences should be such as to participate in the total meaning, which is to say that they should be meaningful in themselves rather than accidental" (98). He maintains in particular that "a medial metrical substitution ought to have the power to persuade us that, given the local pressures of emotion and utterance, it is

2. Paul Fussell, *Poetic Meter and Poetic Form*, rev. ed. (New York: McGraw-Hill, 1979), 119.

entirely *inevitable*" (99, my emphasis). Fussell's principle applies as well to the composition of a metrical translation and may be said to extend by corollary to the notion of a certain translingual inevitability that seems to be the hallmark of a masterful translation. Indeed, since one poem or canto by Baudelaire or Dante can actually yield quite different translations, each of which has the mark of inevitability, I am led to conclude that a brilliant metrical translation is infinitely more complicated than a monolingual poem, for the latter would presumably entail only one inevitable-feeling expression whereas the former obviously might have many because it is the result of a collaborative process combining the creative impulses intrinsic to the original poem and those inherent in the translator's psyche.

APPENDIX

Drafts of the Translation of Du Bellay's *Heureux qui, comme Ulysse, a fait un beau voyage* (*Les Regrets*, Sonnet XXXI)

Heureux qui, comme Ulysse, a fait un beau voyage,
Ou comme cestuy la qui conquit la toison,
Et puis est retourné, plein d'usage & raison,
Vivre entre ses parents le reste de son aage!

Quand revoiray-je, helas, de mon petit village
Fumer la cheminee, & en quelle saison,
Revoiray-je le clos de ma pauvre maison,
Qui m'est une province, et beaucoup d'avantage?

Plus me plaist le sejour qu'ont basty mes ayeux,
Que des palais Romains le front audacieux,
Plus que le marbre dur me plaist l'ardoise fine,

Plus mon Loyre Gaulois que le Tybre Latin,
Plus mon petit Lyré que le mont Palatin,
Et plus que l'air marin la douceur Angevine.

The successful translation of a good formal poem requires talent, of course, but also a great deal of patient and conscientious craftsmanship.

I have in this appendix reproduced some of the drafts involved in the translation of Du Bellay's sonnet, "Heureux qui, comme Ulysse, a fait un beau voyage," discussed in chapter 4. The selected drafts are presented in rough chronological order and most of the individual drafts contain both progressive and retrogressive emendations; a single draft may thus contain many revisions made before the translation is transferred to another page. The many revisions, eliminations, and restorations of discarded elements bear witness to the intense revision process that occurs as the translator bargains with the original poet's muse. Most of these revisions are indecipherable to anyone but me, but they hopefully reveal something about the itinerary of the translation process: that the earliest drafts are the most chaotic and full of fits and starts, self-doubt, and uncertainties; and that as the revisions continue the corrections taper off and in the end involve a very small number of equivocations in which some lingering alternatives were weighed before I decided that I had brought the process as close to an artistic transcreation as I could. Others have done or will no doubt do better. It is the process itself that interested me in chapter 4 and interests me here. The following pages are a log of sorts of the drill explored in chapter 4.

One evening I was reading some poems by Du Bellay and decided to attempt a translation of one of his great poems. I had always liked "Heureux qui, comme Ulysse, a fait un beau voyage" and after rereading it I grabbed a piece of paper on the night table and spent about an hour trying to get a handle on the first stanza, trying out various rhymes, knowing that, for me, the way that a first stanza works out tends to influence the rest of the translation (Fig. 1, p. 97).

That piece of paper became unmanageable and the next day I printed out the poem randomly from the Internet and entered in its margins a rough version of that first draft and continued to do a rough translation of the rest of the sonnet (Fig. 2, p. 98). The next draft I entered into chapter 4, which I was writing, and I continued to revise the typescript, including the poem (Fig. 3, p. 99).

Then I retyped this latest draft double-spaced and continued my revisions on that sheet (Fig. 4) and repeated this process over four revisions from January 28, 2013, through February 3, 2013 (Figs. 4–7, pp. 100–103).

As mentioned in my essay (chapter 4), I am still of two minds regarding the last line, and I feel that the fourth line remains unresolved; but that is fitting because there is no definitive translation, only a sense of inevitability that the translator can reasonably hope to achieve, in accordance with the old adage that the it takes an expert to make something difficult look easy. These facsimiles of drafts are meant only to demonstrate the difficulties in the verse translation process and I am not submitting them as evidence of the expertise requisite to achievement of the proverbial ease.

In compiling and revising this book of essays I vacillated for months between including and omitting the facsimiles of the countless, mostly illegible handwritten revisions that I had made while translating a single formal poem, in this instance a sonnet by Du Bellay.

The preservation of such emendations might come across as egomaniacal and seem bent on elevating the translator's role in the bizarre and intricate symbiotic contract between the source and target texts; however, the duplication of these revisions, rendered largely unreadable by virtue of sequential versions accumulated on the palimpsest, is intended to provide the reader with a sonogram or MRI of the incubation of a verse translation. The facsimiles are not meant to be literally deciphered and read. They should, to the contrary, be considered as the murky slurry of spontaneous creation and intuitive deliberation from which the choicest nuggets of the final translation were panned.

The dedication and patience of the verse translator (the hopeful gold-nugget panner) are seldom appreciated although a poor translation is often little more than a ladleful of slurry.

I decided to retain this odd appendix after perusing a feature in the August 6, 2017, edition of the *New York Times Book Review* in which much is made of five modern poems, duplicating the typescripts that include a few handwritten changes and gratuitous comments made on the typescripts by the authors. We cannot know when the marginal comments were added and the textual revisions are, at best, minimal, as might be expected since the first draft of a genuine poem emerges sui generis from the author's psyche. Those manuscript reproductions actually bolster my contention in several of the above chapters that the symbiotic rigors at play in verse translation entail an incredible number of semantic, syntactic, and esthetic decisions and reconsiderations.

Those actually interested in the dilemmas in creating and revising a literary translation will find a legible version of the "gold panning" process involving another poem detailed in chapter 7, "Baudelaire's 'The Enemy'—Tracking the Revisions."

The Drafts

Figure 1

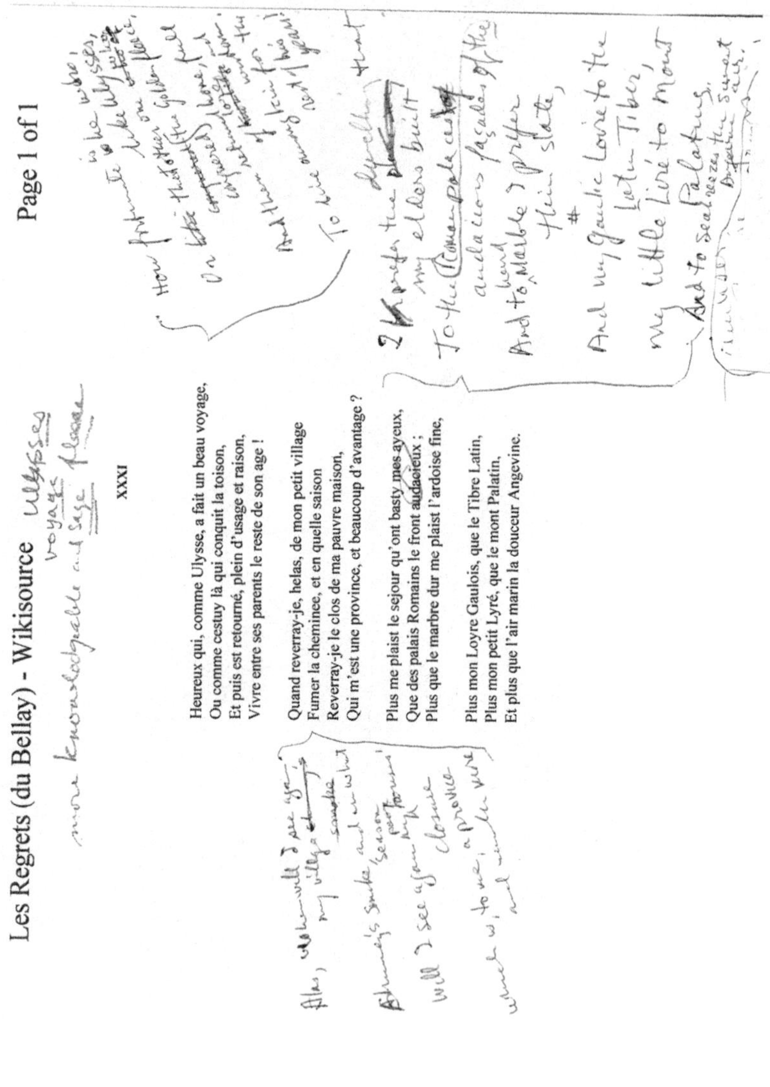

Les Regrets (du Bellay) - Wikisource Page 1 of 1

XXXI

Heureux qui, comme Ulysse, a fait un beau voyage,
Ou comme cestuy là qui conquit la toison,
Et puis est retourné, plein d'usage et raison,
Vivre entre ses parents le reste de son age !

Quand reverray-je, helas, de mon petit village
Fumer la cheminee, et en quelle saison
Reverray-je le clos de ma pauvre maison,
Qui m'est une province, et beaucoup d'avantage ?

Plus me plaist le sejour qu'ont basty mes ayeux,
Que des palais Romains le front audacieux ;
Plus que le marbre dur me plaist l'ardoise fine,

Plus mon Loyre Gaulois, que le Tibre Latin,
Plus mon petit Lyré, que le mont Palatin,
Et plus que l'air marin la douceur Angevine.

Figure 2

Joachim Du Bellay Sonnet XXXI [*Les Regrets*]

Translated by Eric Sellin

How fortunate is he who, like Ulysses
Or like Jason who sailed off to claim the Golden Fleece,
Returns, tested and wiser, from trips overseas
To live out his remaining years among kin in peace.

Alas, when shall I see my village again?
The smoke rising from my chimney? Which season shall find me
Once more back home in my old humble demesne
Whose garden is, to me, a province or vast country?

I far prefer the dwelling my elders called home
To the pompous façades of the palaces of Rome;
And to hard marble slabs I prefer slates thin as wafers,

To the Latin Tiber my Gallic Loire valley,
To Palatine Hill my small town of Liré,
And to the sea breezes the soft Angevin zephyrs.

Figure 3

Du Bellay Sonnet XXXI

[Translated by Eric Sellin (in progress)]

How fortunate is he who, like Ulysses
Or like the one who claimed the Golden Fleece,
Has returned from a fine voyage across the seas
To live out his life among his kin, in peace.

And when shall I ever see my village again,
The smoke rising from my chimney? Which season shall find me
Once again at home in my old humble demesne
Whose garden is, to me, a province or vaster property?

I prefer the dwelling that my forebears builded
To the façades of the Roman palaces, garishly gilded;
And to hard marble I prefer slate thin as wafers,

To the Latin Tiber my Gallic Loire Valley,
To Palatine Hill my little town of Liré,
And to the sea air the soft Angevine zephyrs.

Figure 4

Du Bellay Sonnet XXXI

[Translated by Eric Sellin (in progress)]

Oh, how fortunate is he who, like Ulysses
Or like the one who claimed the Golden Fleece,
Returns, both learned and wise, from trips overseas
To live the rest life among kin, in peace.

Oh, when shall I ever see my village again,
The smoke rising from my chimney? Which season shall find me
Once more at home in my old modest demesne
Whose garden is, to me, a province or vast property?

I far prefer the dwelling that my forebears builded
To the façades of the Roman palaces, garishly gilded;
And to hard marble slabs I prefer slate thin as wafers,

To the Latin Tiber my Gallic Loire Valley,
To Palatine Hill my small village of Liré,
And to the sea air the soft Angevine zephyrs.

Figure 5

Joachim Du Bellay Sonnet XXXI [*Les Regrets*]

Translated by Eric Sellin

Oh, how fortunate is he who, like Ulysses
Or like Jason who sailed off to claim the Golden Fleece,
Returns, experienced and wise, from trips overseas
To live the rest of his life among kin in peace.

Oh, when shall I ever see my village again?
The smoke rising from my chimney? Which season shall find me
Once more back home in my old humble demesne
Whose garden is, to me, a province or vast country?

I prefer by far the dwelling that my forebears called home
To the ostentatious façades of the palaces of Rome;
And to hard marble slabs I prefer slates thin as wafers,

To the Latin Tiber my Gallic Loire Valley,
To Palatine Hill my small town of Liré,
And to the sea breezes the gentle Angevin zephyrs.

Figure 6

Joachim Du Bellay Sonnet XXXI [*Les Regrets*]

Translated by Eric Sellin

How fortunate is he who, like Ulysses
Or like Jason who sailed off to claim the Golden Fleece,
Returns, tested and wiser, from trips overseas
To live out his remaining years among kin in peace.

Alas, when shall I see my village again?
The smoke rising from my chimney? Which season shall find me
Once more back home in my old humble demesne
Whose garden is, to me, a province or vast country?

I prefer ~~by far~~ the dwelling that my forebears called home
To the ostentatious façades of the palaces of Rome,
And to hard marble slabs I prefer slates thin as wafers,

To the Latin Tiber my Gallic Loire Valley,
To Palatine Hill my small town of Liré,
And to the sea breezes the soft Angevin zephyrs.

2/3/13

Figure 7

Final Version (Perhaps!)

Sonnet XXXI [*Les Regrets*]

Joachim Du Bellay

How fortunate is he who, like Ulysses
Or like Jason who sailed off to claim the Golden Fleece,
Returns, tested and wiser, from trips overseas
To live the rest of his life among kin in peace.

Alas, when shall I see my village again?
The smoke rising from my chimney? Which season shall
find me
Once more back home in my old humble demesne
Whose garden is, to me, a province or a country?

I far prefer the dwelling my forebears called home
To all the pompous façades of the palaces in Rome;
And to hard marble slabs I prefer slates thin as wafers,

To the Latin Tiber my Gallic Loire valley,
To Palatine Hill my small town of Liré,
And to the sea breezes the soft Angevin zephyrs.

Eric Sellin, professor emeritus of French at Tulane University, was born and raised in Philadelphia. Before moving to Tulane in 1991, he taught French and comparative literature for twenty-eight years at Temple University. He has also taught English, creative writing, and American literature at the Universities of Pennsylvania, Bordeaux, Algiers, and Dakar.

Sellin's scholarly works include *The Dramatic Concepts of Antonin Artaud* (1968; Quid Pro Books remastered edition, 2017) and *Reflections on the Aesthetics of Futurism, Dadaism, and Surrealism: A Prosody beyond Words* (1993), and more than 150 articles and translations. In addition, Sellin is a poet who writes in English and French. His poetry publications include *Night Voyage* (1964), *Borne kilométrique* (1973), *Dead of Noon* (1992), *Ombres de mon soleil: Poèmes 1970–2005* (2006), and *The Dimming and Other Poems* (2017). He is also the author of two books on soccer and a past editor of two scholarly journals, *CELFAN Review* and *Africana Journal.*

Sellin retired in 2001 and since 2006 has resided in Philadelphia where he devotes most of his time to reading light fiction and to writing and translating poetry. Sellin's and Mbarek Sryfi's co-translation from French of Abdelfattah Kilito's *Arabs and the Art of Storytelling: A Strange Familiarity*, published by Syracuse University Press in 2014, was a finalist for the 28th French-American Foundation Translation Prize in nonfiction (2015), and their co-translation from Arabic of *The Blueness of the Evening: Selected Poems of Hassan Najmi* was published by the University of Arkansas Press in 2018.